For Steve

What Works at Work

A Guide for Thoughtful Managers

What Works at Work
A Guide for Thoughtful Managers

Mark O'Sullivan

The Starbank Press
2014

What Works at Work was published in 2014 by The Starbank Press
at 58 Greenway Lane, Bath, Somerset BA2 4LL

A CIP record for this book
is available from the British Library
ISBN 978-0-9569812-1-9

Also by Mark O'Sullivan:
Britanniae (Starbank Press, Bath, 2011)

*The Starbank Press is an imprint of Resource Synergies Ltd,
58 Greenway Lane, Bath, Somerset BA2 4LL*

CONTENTS

Preface

This slim book runs over the main areas of people-management and seeks to offer managers a brief guide, written in ordinary language rather than some impenetrable mid-Atlantic jargon, which will help them see the wood from the trees when looking at some fundamental challenges. Chapter 1 explains a bit more at whom the book is aimed, and why they might want to read it.

However, you ought to have my basic assumptions at the start. I believe that how people are managed at work is important, since it is one of the main influences on our standard of living, and since most of us spend half our lives in our jobs and need to know that we are not wasting our time. I believe social science gives us quite a lot of real knowledge of what works in management and what does not, and that we ought to try and do the things that work and avoid those that do not. And I believe that, because people are complicated, their organisations are complex too, so that it's important not just to grasp at what looks like the obvious solution to a problem, but to try carefully to think through all the ramifications before taking action.

My thanks are due to David Guest and his team at Birkbeck who first guided me through the jungle of management science; to my colleagues in organisations, mainly in the civil service, who provided a wealth of practical examples of how management should (and shouldn't) be done; to the members of the Association for Business Psychology, who have remained loyal to the cause of evidence-based management, despite the deafening marketing hype of popular management gurus; and to the taxpayer, who funded a series of excellent courses at the Civil Service College, led by Julian Rizzello and others, which did more than most to enable me to reflect on the world of organisations and my experience of it.

Mark O'Sullivan
Bath, Somerset
January 2014

About the author

After reading Classics as a scholar at Cambridge, Mark O'Sullivan joined the Department of the Environment, serving in a range of policy advice roles and supporting Michael Heseltine's introduction of new business methods known as *Management Information for Ministers*. Subsequently he assisted with the Financial Management Initiative, including, as head of the Finance Division in the 20,000-strong Property Services Agency, the introduction there of commercial accounting.

In 1989 he moved to the Scottish Office, initially to the finance team, and set out to get practical qualifications with a MSc in Organisational Behaviour from Birkbeck College London, a diploma from the Association of Chartered Certified Accountants, and Fellowship of the Chartered Institute of Personnel & Development. In Scotland he handled policy on the environment and on education, set up central services in the new Nature Conservancy Council for Scotland, reviewed governance in the Scottish Examination Board, and led analysis of the staffing changes required for the new Scottish Government.

He returned to England to an international post in DEFRA, and subsequently moved across to local government as a director in the Cambridgeshire County Council. He left the public sector in 2005 for consultancy work advising public, private and third sectors, primarily on leadership, project management and organisational change. In 2012 he stepped down after 8 years as a director of the Association of Business Psychologists; he currently sits on the Rural Economy Sector Group of the West of England Local Enterprise Partnership, and holds a Ministerial appointment on the Cotswolds Conservation Board.

Mr O'Sullivan, a Londoner by birth, lives in Bath. He has written in a number of professional works, most recently *Retaining School Leaders: a guide to keeping talented leaders engaged* (National College for School Leadership, 2007). In 2008 he edited a work of fiction by the late Richard Ogden, *Inquiry into an Unknown Planet*, and in 2011 he published a historical novel, *Britanniae*.

Chapter 1: Why you need this book

This book is different. No, really. Let me explain.

If you go into an airport bookshop, you will see a lot of books for managers. Most of them tell you stories about how it has been done somewhere else.

Often they have sensible advice. But when you read them you usually realise that they are not about you. You see that the way your own organisation is structured, the way it is led, the atmosphere in the office, how people are recruited and trained, how what people do is rewarded – all these are different in your office from the way they are in those books. So you think, "Well, it may have worked there for him[1]. But, with all those differences, how could it work here for me?"

You are asking a good question. Management researchers have worked away industriously for something like a century now, but they still cannot agree on how organisations should be run, or what you need to do to make them successful. So you would be right in thinking that something funny is going on. Are the authors just touting for more business, like the outside experts who come in and do an expensive study, and then come to the conclusion that more consultancy work is needed? Well, maybe there is a bit of that[2]. But there is more to it too; and, if you go on reading, I hope to show you what.

You might think that there's a right answer to every management question. Once upon a time, nearly everyone thought that. Management theory grew out of a military background, one where people like to know clearly what's

---

[1] They do tend to be "him"...
[2] cf Micklethwaite J and Wooldridge A, 1996, *The Witch Doctors*, Heinemann, London, pp 49-68.

what, and it was given its biggest boost at the turn of the last century by an American army engineer called Frederick W. Taylor.

Taylor's were the days of H. G. Wells and Jules Verne, of the magic of electricity and the steam turbine, a time when (how unimaginable!) messages could be sent instantly, by…vacuum tube. In those days, it was common to think of science as revealing the unambiguous Truth and the absolute Reality. Taylor was driven by romantic dreams of entrepreneurial progress, as well as of the United States' Puritan roots. And he claimed to have discovered *scientific management*, the "one best way to organise". He had a vision of organisations and their workers as machines with a myriad complex parts, and their expert managers as operators controlling them in every detail. Scientists were like the priests of ancient Egypt, governing all real access to knowledge; and managers, to Taylor, were going to be the priests of the 20th Century.

Taylor has had a huge following, and still has gigantic influence. Nevertheless, he has also been described as "a disturbed personality" and "one of the most criticised of all organisation theorists"[3]. Indeed, one expert has gone so far as to say "the sheer silliness of many of his ideas, and the barbarities they led to when applied, encourage ridicule and denunciation"[4]. And to begin with, it's important to realise that, when you have a management question, there often *isn't* a single right answer.

Indeed, as it turned out, Taylor's way was not so evidently the "one best way to organise". No sooner had his ideas started gathering pace in the USA, than an alternative view emerged in Britain, proposed by a Cambridge academic, C. S. Myers.

[3] Morgan G, 1986, *Images of Organisation*, Sage, London pp 29-30.
[4] Rose M, 1975, *Industrial Behaviour: theoretical development since Taylor*, Penguin Books, Harmondsworth p 31.

Challenged to account for unexpected cases of fatigue and boredom among soldiers, which had alarmed generals and politicians in the First World War, Myers set up a National Institute of Industrial Psychology. And that began the work of what has become known as the "human factor school", which took a very different and much broader view of what makes people tick than Taylor's had, and has since influenced a range of successor movements and institutions[5].

Nor is this the only alternative to Taylorism. Indeed, one survey has set out in detail no fewer than ten competing theoretical models for thinking about and acting in organisations, describing them as things ranging from machines, political systems or cultures, to organisms, psychic prisons, and flux[6].

This doesn't mean, of course, that there are no right answers to management problems. But people and organisations are complicated, and it does mean that right answers are often hard to spot, that sometimes there is more than one right answer, and that sometimes the least wrong answer is the best you can hope for. You do need to be well-informed, to keep your wits about you, and to know when to trust your common sense.

Another important thing to bear in mind is that the quality of what is written about management really does vary a great deal. Some books are written by successful, wealthy, self-opinionated businessmen, with limited scientific knowledge and an appetite for publicity. These can be a good read. They can be inspiring. But, if you think about it, of course, the idea that what worked for Henry Ford will

---

[5] Rose M, 1975, *Industrial Behaviour: theoretical development since Taylor*, Penguin Books, Harmondsworth p 67 and Parts 3 and 4.

[6] Morgan G, 1986, *Images of Organisation*, Sage, London (no, even after reading his brilliant book I'm still not very sure what he means by "flux" in this context, though it does sound good).

work for you too could well be no more than a wild hope. And it's not just eccentric geniuses who espouse it. As I write this I'm looking at a copy of *People Management* with an article[7] about the management style used by the successful restaurant chain Wagamama – with the implication that readers will find it works for them too. That may fit with the celebrity culture, but in fact it has nothing to do with good management: a good manager will use techniques which have been shown to work for a situation which is similar in relevant respects to his own.

Even very famous academics sometimes write books based on what they assume to be the case, rather than what has been shown to be fact by robust research and statistical analysis. Now, it is true that people who have spent a lifetime thinking about organisations have often acquired a great deal of wisdom about them; and the development of theory can certainly be very important even when it is not open to proof. But, as Copernicus, Darwin and Einstein showed (each in his own way), there is always a difference between the voice of experience, however authoritative, and conclusions reached after sound scientific work; and sometimes what looks like common sense turns out to be nonsense.

Moreover, there are sticky problems with organisational research, problems that are hard to exclude and that do not seem to go away. Most importantly, studies in the social sciences are much more complex than demonstrations of Boyle's Law, since it is often impossible to control for externalities. At the most general level, it is inescapable that human society is very complicated: as a result, the rationality of people's decision-making is always limited, because there are important parts of their situation which they can never thoroughly understand[8].

---

[7] 15 June 2006 p 32.

[8] March J G and Simon H A, 1958, *Organizations*, Blackwell, Oxford.

There are more specific problems too. For example, as often as not, the raw material that academics have to hand is their students, so a lot of psychological experiments have always used students as their subjects[9]. This may be no problem where the work is on visual perception. But when it is on interviewing techniques, do we really have grounds to think that teenage psychology students with little experience of work or life will react the same way as (say) forty-year-old managers in the processed food industry? On the other hand, attempts to use the results of real-life consultancy work for research are very often thwarted, since the firms studied have the reasonable fear that publishing details of what they do might tell their competitors things which they really do not want them to know.

Another problem is that psychological research has traditionally focused on individuals, often because there it is easier to control their experimental environment: and psychologists' default mode, therefore, is to look at individual differences and reactions. But, actually, most important things about the workplace happen not to isolated individuals, but within a social system. This is much more complicated and more expensive to study, and the amount of academic time, money and effort available is limited. Hence these vital issues of how social events influence what happens at work are often poorly researched.

Again, because the USA is five times the size of Britain, and richer to boot, a lot of the published research is done in America. Of course the two countries have a common heritage, and mostly share a language, and we have been soaking up Hollywood films for several generations, so they *are* pretty similar. But there are also obvious big differ-

---

[9] Now see Heinrich J, Heine S J and Norenzayan A, 2010, "The weirdest people in the world?", *Behavioral and Brain Sciences* Vol 33 Issue 2-3, pp 61-83. Note too that leadership studies have often for obvious reasons been funded by the US armed forces, and use servicemen as their subjects, which gives rise to additional doubts about how representative they are.

ences (think religion, or guns, or the NHS). Indeed, most firms publishing psychometric tests, usually American, have found it necessary to develop special versions for the UK. So it is risky to make assumptions that results which are valid in the USA are also valid in Europe. But, pressured by time and cost, people often do just that[10].

Finally, a word of caution about common sense. We all laugh at the time and effort wasted by social scientists who labour to prove that children like to eat chocolate, or that bereaved people get sad. But though the obvious is often true, common sense is not always a good guide. A major step forward in the 1960s was when psychology started to develop a catalogue of ways in which people often or always misunderstand the world. For example, people tend to think their own successes are down to their ability, and their failures to their circumstances; to link the failures of others to their abilities, when it is circumstances that are to blame; and to exaggerate how much other people agree with them, or how much other people notice what they do. Such biases warp people's judgement, and lead to poor decisions[11].

Compare the case of medicine. Most doctors are rightly committed to evidence-based medicine, driven by scientific findings. But they also know that they have to work in a real world where not every patient is suffering from a

---

[10] A few differences in a little more detail: in 2007 capital punishment was favoured by 69% of Americans but only 50% of Britons (Grey E *et al.*, 2007, *Attitudes to the death penalty*, Ipsos Mori); in 1998/99 internet advertising was thought to be (i) informative and (ii) trustworthy by 62% and 48% respectively of Americans, but only 46% and 37% of Britons (Mojsa M and Rettie R, 2003, *Attitudes to Internet Advertising: A Cross-Cultural Comparison*, Kingston University Occasional Paper Series No 54); the proportion of people blaming obesity on food companies or the government, rather than saying it's the fault of obese people, is around twice as high in Britain as in America (study by the McCann-Erickson group of advertising agencies reported on www.foodnavigator-usa.com on 7 July 2004).
[11] Heider F, 1958, *The psychology of interpersonal relations*, New York, Wiley; Kahneman D, Slovic P and Tversky A, 1982, *Judgment under Uncertainty: Heuristics and Biases*.

disease for which there is a proven effective treatment, and that, for many, the treatments which have been found useful in the past are worth using again, even if there are as yet no double-blind-controlled trials to prove their effectiveness beyond doubt.

Equally, in the world of business, managers will often come across situations in which there is no demonstrably right course of action. In such cases they too need to use their experience and their intuition. However, when they find that there is real, hard evidence to guide them, then they are unprofessional if they do not let that rule their judgement.

Of course, it is not easy to tell the sound, evidence-based advice from the froth of self-important puffery. That can often take a lot of research for which busy managers do not have time[12]. The modest aims of this book are (i) to flag up the circumstances where management has been more successful as a science, and to help the reader to get a feel for when one might look to rely on authoritative findings; and (ii) where there is no robust empirical basis for decisions, to give a bit of background about where the conventional wisdom in such cases has come from, and offer some suggestions about what sort of action might make sense.

Do not be put off by these warnings: they are not there to rubbish an important discipline, but to counter some of the bombastic assertions which are too often made. For we

---

[12] Appeals to improve communication between the academy and the manager's office have been in vain: Rousseau D M and McCarthy S, 2007, "Educating Managers From an Evidence-Based Perspective", *Academy of Management Learning & Education*, vol 6 no 1 pp 84-101. Recently, even HR managers, when asked to identify well-established management research findings, answered 43% of the test questions wrong in America and 38% in Holland: Rynes S, Colbert A & Brown K, 2002, "HR professionals' beliefs about effective human resource practices: correspondence between research and practice", *Human Resource Management*, vol 41 pp 149-174; Sanders K, van Riemsdijk M, & Groen B, 2008, "The gap between research and practice: A replication study of HR professionals' beliefs about effective human resource practices", *International Journal of Human Resource Management*, vol 19 pp 1976-88.

do know a lot about what works at work, if not quite as much as some people claim[13]. Let's start where people begin in organisations: let's start by looking at recruitment and selection.

---

[13] The extent of disagreement among leading academics was recently surveyed by Guest D and Zijlstra F R H, 2012, "Academic perceptions of the research evidence base in work and organizational psychology: A European perspective", *Journal of Occupational and Organizational Psychology*, 85, 542–555.

Chapter 2: Recruitment

This chapter looks at the strengths and weaknesses of the methods used to select people for recruitment, promotion, training and redundancy, including interviews, assessment centres, work sampling, curricula vitæ, psychometric tests and handwriting analysis. It warns of the dangers of subjectivity and not being clear about what is needed. It touches on selection for potential, and on the radical approach of random selection.

> *There had been a showy addition to Mr Oates' furniture since Guy Crouchback's last visit; an elaborate machine of more modern construction than any permanent exhibit in the room commandeered from the Museum.*
>
> *"What have you got there?"*
>
> *Mr Oates made a little grimace of gratification.*
>
> *"Ah! You have found my tender spot. You might call it my pet. Absolutely new. It's just been flown in from America. It took 560 man-hours to install. The mechanics came from America, too. There isn't another like it in the country."*
>
> *"But what is it?"*
>
> *"An electronic personnel selector."*
>
> *"Have we any electronic personnel?"*
>
> *"It covers every contingency. For example, suppose I want to find a lieutenant-colonel who is a long-distance swimmer, qualified as a barrister, with experience of catering in tropical countries, instead of going through all the records I just press these buttons: one, two, three, four, and..." There was a whirring noise from the depths of the engine, a series of clicks as though from a slot-machine telling fortunes on a pier, and a card shot up. "You see – totally blank – that means negative."*
>
> *"I think I could have guessed that."*
>
> *"Yes, I was illustrating an extreme example. Now here" – he picked up a chit from his tray – "is a genuine enquiry. I've been asked to find an officer for special employment; under 40, with a university degree, who has lived in Italy, and had commando training – one, two, three, four, five –" whirr, click, click, click, click, click. "Here we are. And that is a remarkable coincidence."*
>
> *The card he held bore the name of A/Ty Captain Crouchback G., RC, att. HOO HQ. Guy did not attempt to correct the machine on the point of his age, or on the extent of his commando training.*
>
> *"I seem the only one."*
>
> *"Yes. I don't know what it's for, of course, but I will send your name in at once."*
>
> *Sword of Honour, Evelyn Waugh, 1961*

Key message of this chapter: Selection methods for recruitment, promotion, training and redundancy have been robustly evaluated. You cannot expect always to get your decisions right, but you can be confident whether the methods you are using are good ones or bad ones.

Whether in the private, public or third sector, all organisations exist to deliver goods or services, of one sort or another. For this, they need productive assets, and increasingly these are not buildings and machines, but people – enough people, of course, and not too many, but also, crucially, people with the right skills.

Recruit-ment: general

We get the skills needed for an effective organisation by getting in the right people (and sometimes getting out the wrong ones), or else by training and education. And at the individual level, staff can be moved, or adjustments made to the shape of jobs, so that each role fits its occupant better. But recruitment is where it all starts. In tight labour markets the problem is finding candidates for jobs, and employers may have to take what they can get[14]; but more often the problem is selection.

Unfortunately, we are not good at selection. It is fair to say that we have not advanced beyond the situation described in a major report twenty-five years ago which condemned our complacency, remarking that the methods we generally use give too much weight to subjective judge-ments which are unreliable and inconsistent: and observed that by taking on a new recruit, a line manager is too often making a public statement of faith in that person which must then be defended at all costs, however poorly they perform[15]. This is not because psychological science has failed. It is because we do not use it[16]. And that is a pity, since selection is actually the area of people management

---

[14] Keep E and James S, 2010, *Recruitment and Selection – the Great Neglected Topic*, SKOPE Research Paper No. 88, ESRC Centre on Skills, Knowledge and Organisational Performance, Cardiff University & University of Oxford, p 5.

[15] Bevan S and Fryatt J, 1988, *Employee Selection in the UK* (IMS Report no. 160), Institute of Manpower Studies, Brighton, p 66.

[16] And, as it has been pointed out, "There is a depressing reluctance, which seems to be common across contemporary UK social science, to ignore work if it was under-taken more than a few years ago. A great deal of very useful research on recruitment and selection was undertaken in the 1970s, 80s and 90s, but has vanished from sight and citation. This is unfortunate. Some of the data it reports may no longer be relevant (though it can offer interesting contrasts with conditions today), but many of the typologies, models and analytical frameworks and perspectives generated in these forgotten studies remain valid and useful." – Keep E and James S, 2010, *op. cit.*, p 2.

where we have some of the best scientific answers about what really works, and what does not.

In selection there is an elementary need, to begin with, to be crystal clear about the content of the job you want to fill. If you're not, then you really have no basis for deciding what sort of person can do it and what sort can't (though it's surprising how many people fudge this simple question[17]). Remember too that once you employ someone it will often be difficult and costly to get rid of them, so getting it right is important: this is a decision which you *must* give care and effort to, whatever the level of the new employee. If you go looking for "someone who is good at writing Excel scripts", when what you really want is someone who can produce a spreadsheet to automate the monthly sales projections, the task may need someone who can negotiate carefully with the admin staff who are doing the job at the moment; the danger is that you will appoint a geek who will get up their noses, and cause his line manager endless bother and heartache.

It is also important not to over-specify the content and re-quirements of a job. For one is not always looking for the "best" candidate. People who are too good for the job will soon become demoralised and disruptive: one study mentions a successful retailer who in the end found it best to give aptitude tests to applicants for shop assistant jobs, then to appoint the candidates scoring *lowest* in the tests, on the grounds that the jobs were so limited and tedious that any-one with any real ability would soon become bored and leave[18].

---

[17] As the engineer Steve Hoddell has remarked, "It is a salutary thought that working to rule is a powerful tool for unions to use to put pressure on employers. Since this merely involves doing the job as specified, it is difficult to avoid the conclusion that whoever specified the job did not do it particularly well".

[18] Beynon H, Grimshaw D, Rubbery J and Ward K, 2002, *Managing Employment Change – the New Realities of Work*, OUP, Oxford.

Fashions in selection methods come and go, an important reason being that, even though our knowledge is comparatively good in this area, all the same no process is anywhere near foolproof. Hence – just to side-step for a moment – it is worth paying attention to what colleagues think: if for some reason they have a prejudice against a certain method, they may mistrust an appointment made through it, and this may get the appointee off to a poor start which is never recovered.

But some methods of assessment are certainly better than others. And there are those that are much worse. Thus, there is no decent evidence that handwriting tests work at all, for example. Or age. Or astrology. Or the size of a candidate's ears[19].

Usually there are three ways of assessing people for employment: *interview*, *work sample* and *psychometric tests*. All of these have variations, and all have costs. Often the most reliable results come by combining them, since, while none of them is particularly accurate, the ways they are defective are different, so that one may compensate for the weaknesses of another[20].

Studies have found that in selection a simple interview tends to be little more than one-third more successful than random[21]. This is hard to believe, because we all think we

---

[19] "Psychological consultant Dr. John P. Foley Jnr. of New York City relates that a top executive of a client company confided to him, 'John, a good executive should have big ears'. Dr Foley added that he immediately noticed that his informant had 'pretty big ears'." (Packard V, 1965, *The Pyramid Climbers*, Penguin, Harmondsworth, p. 107). On age, see now Inceoglu I, Segers J and Bartram D, 2012, "Age-related differences in work motivation", *Journal of Occupational and Organizational Psychology*, 85, 300–329.

[20] This is the basis of the "assessment centre" approach used now in many selection processes, especially for graduates, for management roles and in the public sector.

[21] The main reason is presumably that any scoring systems used are ultimately subject to the human biases of the people assessing the candidate (Brown P and Hesketh P, 2004, *The Mismanagement of Talent*, OUP, Oxford). This can be improved a bit by good structuring of an interview, but nevertheless is no more effective, and rather

are fantastic judges of people and can sum them up at a glance. That isn't true, and we need to go on telling ourselves this, even though we do get so very flattered by being in the interviewer role which seems to tell us that it is.

You can improve the effectiveness of an interview process by using more interviews or interviewers (perhaps including potential team members), training the interviewers and structuring the interviews sensibly, and establishing very clear criteria against which to make the decision.

Interviews tend to discriminate against nervous candidates for jobs, especially when stress is not a big issue in the job itself. But, unlike other assessment processes, they do enable you to assess the emotional chemistry of what it would be like working with this person. And my private guess is that, where recruitment is for a particular post (rather than, say, a trainee grade in a big firm), a significant proportion of decisions are in fact swung by the reaction of the line manager at the interview. Though it ought to go without saying that it is important to avoid appointing people simply on the basis that their "face fits".

There is a fashion at present for competency-based interviewing, which means asking people to describe in detail how they have behaved in the past in specific situations which could come up in the job. This is a good method, and in principle it does improve the success of interviewing, so that you are around 50% more likely than random to find someone who can do the job well[22].

---

more expensive, than the simple use of biodata (e.g. studying someone's *curriculum vitæ*) – Schmidt F L and Hunter J E, 1998, "The Validity and Utility of Selection Methods in Personnel Psychology: Practical and Theoretical Implications of 85 Years of Research Findings", *Psychological Bulletin* vol 124 no 2 pp 262-274; see also Robertson I T and Smith M, 2001, "Personnel Selection", *Journal of Occupational and Organizational Psychology*, vol 74 pp 441-472. On biodata see further page 16 below.

[22] Rynes S, Barber A, and Varma G, 2000, 'Research on the employment interview', in Cooper G and Locke E (*edd.*), *Industrial and Organizational Psychology: Linking Theory and Practice*, Blackwell, Oxford.

But success using it does depend on your being good at identifying relevant situations, and the candidate not freezing up through nerves. And more seriously, even when the candidate has all the right skills to deal with the situations you challenge them with, they may not have met those situations in the past, whether because they haven't yet done that sort of job, or because you just happen to pick particular incidents which they never experienced. If this is the case, then they are likely to fail the selection process, even though they could do the job really well. That may be a price you're happy to pay, because of the risk of employing the wrong person. But if there's a shortage of good candidates, then competency-based interviewing may be cutting off your nose to spite your face[23].

A practical point is that it is really important not to overload interviewers, since after a while making interview decisions they may start rejecting acceptable candidates[24]. Other points about the interview process are that interviewers usually find it easier to decide to reject someone than to accept them, but that when they do decide to reject them they are more likely to be right[25]. An average

---

[23] The technique, of course, discriminates particularly against young people with little work experience, which has led a number of employers such as Nestlé to prefer strengths-based interviewing (*Recruiting Young People: top tips for employers*, CIPD April 2013, p. 5), though this does not have such a strong pedigree.

[24] An interesting study has found that favourable decisions by judges hearing parole applications fell by half after about half a dozen cases, though a meal break restored initial performance: this was thought to be due not to simple tiredness but to decision fatigue: Danziger S, Levav J and Avnaim-Pesso L, 2011, "Extraneous factors in judicial decisions", *Proceedings of the National Academy of Sciences of the United States of America*, published online 11 April 2011. The study has not yet been replicated, but suggests that similar bias may well apply to selection decisions in organisations.

[25] Springbett B M, 1958, "Factors affecting the final decision in the employment interview", *Canadian Journal of Psychology*, vol 12 pp 13-22; Bolster B I and Springbett B M, 1961, "The reaction of interviewers to favorable and unfavorable information", *Journal of Applied Psychology* vol 45 pp 97-103; Carlson R E and Mayfield E C, 1967, "Evaluating interview and employment application data", *Personnel Psychology* vol 20 pp 441-60 (both quoted in Peter B Warr, 1971,

candidate interviewed just after an excellent one may seem poorer than in fact he is, though this is unlikely to be a serious problem[26].

And here's a final thought about choosing selection panels: a good liar may be better than a bad liar at spotting other people lying...[27]

Work sample means that you give people a task that they would meet on the job and see how well they do. It is often thought of in terms of relatively straightforward skill tests: an admin officer might be asked to copy and bind a report or to type up some handwritten notes, a mechanic might be asked to change a set of brake pads or spot why an engine won't start.

Recruit-ment: work sample

But in practice it is used much more widely. This can be on a role-playing basis. A group of candidates may be asked to role-play a committee meeting, each given a certain objective, and scored not just against how well they achieve that, but also against how well they place themselves against the other players for any follow up (negotiation skills, avoiding rows, &c). Or candidates can be given an in-box exercise, where they are put in front of a computer and given a set of emails to reply to within a demanding time limit (maybe interrupted by a phone call from time to time), the responses then being scored according to pre-set criteria. Or an actor can be brought in to role-play a difficult

"Judgements about People at Work", in Warr P B (ed), *Psychology at Work*, first edition, Penguin Books, Harmondsworth, p 225).

[26] Carlson R E, 1970, "Effect of applicant sample on ratings of valid information in an employment setting", *Journal of Applied Psychology* vol 54 pp 217-22; Hakel M D, Ohnesorge J P and Dunnette M D, 1970, "Interviewer evaluations of job applicants' résumés as a function of the qualifications of the immediately preceding applicants", *Journal of Applied Psychology* vol 54 pp 27-30.

[27] Wright G, Berry C, and Bird G, 2012, " 'You can't kid a kidder': association between production and detection of deception in an interactive deception task", *Frontiers in Human Neuroscience*, 6 DOI: http://dx.doi.org/10.3389/fnhum.2012.00087.

customer or other stakeholder, and the interaction observed and scored.

Again, it can be on a work-trial basis. This is especially common in the construction and hospitality industries, where a worker will be taken on briefly to do a task like bricklaying or sandwich-making, and confirmed in the job if they make the grade. Apprenticeships were the classic mode of this approach, and though those are now much less common in the UK than they were, a similar function is currently provided by the growing practice of internships[28].

Though some such assessments can be done on-line or using video-recordings[29], significant supervisory staff input is often needed, and time and cost may limit what is feasible in a particular case. But work sample, if good examples can be used, is one of the best ways of assessment. Studies show it is likely to be about two-thirds better than random[30]. And it may be less likely to discriminate against shyer participants, who, if they can let themselves relax into the role-play, may lose their self-consciousness for a while. The higher costs of these methods are usually much more than offset by their greater accuracy.

Biodata – records of someone's past experience or performance – can be seen as a rather different kind of work sample. They include traditional methods such as references, qualifications, personal recommendations[31] and *curricula vitæ*. More recently, the field has widened to

---

[28] See Keep E and James S, 2010, *op. cit.*, p 15; internships are of course criticised on equal opportunities grounds, and for similar reasons may not always lead to the best potential candidate being appointed.
[29] Anders G, 2011, "The Games They Make You Play", *The Guardian Work supplement* 29 October 2011 pp 1-2, citing recent use by Amazon, Facebook, Citigroup, Société Générale and Genentech.
[30] Schmidt F L and Hunter J E, 1998, *op. cit.* The figure here assumes that it is used in combination with another method such as a general mental ability test, though even without that addition work sample is still the most effective method of all. It is important to be wary, of course, that work sample will not assess potential.
[31] A large sector, especially for low-skilled jobs: Keep E and James S, 2010, *op. cit.*, pp 7-12.

include social networking websites. These have been used by employees to find job advertising and to research working conditions in likely employers, as well as by organisations to identify potential candidates and to investigate the behaviour and discretion applicants show in their private lives.

Some of these latter approaches in particular are invaluable in widening the field of candidates for specialist posts, since they allow one to reach people who are not currently looking for a move (LinkedIn Recruiter, which allows search by particular skills or experience, is especially adapted to this). But one needs to be wary: in general such techniques are by no means as robust as live performance tests, since they can often be easily faked[32], and there are various reasons why referees may wish to modify their reports[33].

There are obvious ethical issues involved (the HR Director for Rent-A-Car Europe has remarked "it is like going into somebody's house and searching through their cupboards"[34]). Moreover, such methods lack the discipline of allowing the candidate the right of reply, and can tempt recruiters towards the use of inappropriate criteria. Those Facebook photos of a drunken night out may look unappealing, but they don't necessarily offer fair evidence of how he behaves at work, and one may lose out on an excellent employee by relying on them. There are other risks of narrowing the field with such methods (in 2009, 30% of the population were still not using the internet), and further

---

[32] Though I suppose that some, if filling a sales vacancy, might think persuasive faking a virtue…

[33] Even qualifications are not always to be relied on, since they do not always measure what is really wanted, and their use in practice seems to be changing over time: see an interesting discussion in Keep E and James S, 2010, *op. cit.*, pp 7-12; also Pellizzari M, 2010, "Do Friends and Relatives Really Help in Getting a Good Job?", Industrial and Labor Relations Review, vol 63 no 3, pp 494-510.

[34] http://www.ceridian.co.uk/connection/articles/recruiting-ethically/ [accessed Oct 2013].

ones of mistaken identity and potentially costly discrimination cases. So far, compared with people abroad, British employers and employees have been very wary of using these approaches[35]. And there has so far been almost no research in this area.

Bear in mind, however, that it is less easy to disguise the truth within small communities. References can be effective, for example, within a particular professional group in a limited geographic area, especially if details can be probed by telephone.

Recruitment: psychometric tests

Psychometric tests have been becoming more popular in recent years. This may be because they are less effort for the employer, since they reduce the time staff have to "waste" holding interviews, or devising and assessing work samples. They are also attractive to consultants, who get from them lucrative work which can be processed by fairly low-paid staff. Further, they project a comforting image of hard science and objectivity – though this may be illusory.

Tests are essentially in two categories. There are tests of specific skills, such as literacy or numeracy or general intelligence. These tend to be well constructed and reliable; they often assess aspects of ability which could be addressed using work sample, but in a more systematic and robust way. They are much more useful than many people seem to think.

The most important to think about relates to general intelligence (identified in 1904, and also known as general mental ability). This is among *the most effective* predictors of suitability for complex jobs[36], though even for managerial

---

[35] Aquent Orange Book 2008-09.
[36] Schmidt F L and Hunter J E, 1998, *op. cit.*: the research giving this result is American, but based on work involving over 32,000 employees in 515 widely varied civilian jobs, and well founded.

or professional roles its usefulness is not as much as two-thirds better than random. Unsurprisingly, for unskilled jobs it is not a great deal of use. It is worth bearing in mind that general intelligence, one of the best predictors of performance for most jobs, can to some extent be improved by training[37].

It used to be thought that one of the virtues of the concept of general intelligence was that it was, indeed, general, and therefore simple to conceptualise and easy to test robustly. In the 1960s this doctrine was challenged by the suggestion that one could distinguish abstract intelligence ("fluid intelligence") from the practical ability to solve problems within one's own culture or situation ("crystallised intelligence")[38]. It has since been argued that one can also separate out practical and creative problem-solving skills as different kinds of intelligence[39]; and even that that the ability to recognise the emotions of oneself or others, to understand social situations, to negotiate relationships and to use one's emotions creatively constitutes another kind of problem-solving skill or intelligence, which has been called "emotional intelligence"[40]. There is little good data as yet about the effectiveness of using these ideas in selection tests.

---

[37] This was for many years not believed to be so, and is clearly not easy, but has been recently shown to be the case: see Klingberg T, 2010, *Trends in Cognitive Sciences,* vol 14 no 7 pp 317-324 and references therein.

[38] Horn J L & Cattell R B, 1966, "Refinement and test of the theory of fluid and crystallized general intelligence", *Journal of Educational Psychology*, vol 57(5), pp 253-270.

[39] Gardner H, 1983, *Frames of Mind: The Theory of Multiple Intelligences*, Basic Books; Sternberg R J, 1985, *Beyond IQ: A triarchic theory of human intelligence*, Cambridge University Press.

[40] Goleman D, 1996, *Emotional Intelligence*, Bloomsbury, London. Though "EQ" has become very popular, many psychometricians are sceptical: the jury is still out, though a good, succinct demolition job, with references, was done by Munro A, 2011, "Emotional Intelligence: extravagant hype or a damaging folly?", *Assessment and Development Matters*, vol 3 no 4 pp 15-17.

Then there are the personality tests. These may be the well-known general tests of personality trait, such as the Myers-Briggs Type Indicator, the 16PF or NEO. They may be a team-role assessment, such as the Belbin Team-Role Self-Perception Inventory, or the Margerison-McCall Team Management Profile. Or they may be tests directed at particular aspects of the personality, such as FIRO-B (which focuses on control and dependency issues), TKI (which looks at preferred approaches to conflict) or the Strong Interest Inventory (used for career counselling).

In recent years, personality tests have been spreading in recruitment selection, and they are now in routine use in about a fifth of workplaces[41]. And there is good evidence that one of the five personality dimensions which they rely on, known as "conscientiousness", is strongly associated with job performance[42]. However, many psychologists think that personality tests are unsuited for recruitment, and that in the work context they should be pretty well exclusively kept for training and development.

They do have a number of problems. A great deal of care and thoroughness, along with advanced statistics, goes into validating these tests, and most of them are very good at doing what they seek to do. But some, even some of the best known, do have technical weaknesses (one of the most popular, for example, the MBTI, has a poor consistency re-cord – so that, if you take the test twice over, you can expect to get the same result not more than two times in three, and perhaps as little as one time in four[43]). Such questions,

---

[41] Keep E and James S, 2010, *op. cit.*, p 16, citing WERS.
[42] Barrick M R and Mount M K, 1991, "The Big Five personality dimensions and job performance: a meta-analysis", *Personnel Psychology*, vol 44, pp 1-26 (the so-called Big Five – Extraversion, Emotional Stability, Agreeableness, Conscientiousness and Openness to Experience – have been more or less agreed upon by psychologists since the 1980s; in an earlier version of the schema there were four).
[43] Commission on Behavioral and Social Sciences and Education, 1991, *In the Mind's Eye: Enhancing Human Performance*, The National Academies Press: the charac-teristic in question is known in the jargon as the test-retest record. This US

though, are not the main problem. The real issue is not whether the tests are measuring things well, so much as whether what they are successfully measuring is actually much use in selection.

Personality tests will score someone against the five dimensions of personality, such as, for example, introvert-extravert. However, if someone comes out on this dimension with a relatively high introversion score, that does not mean that they cannot operate effectively in work contexts which require extraverted behaviour, such as addressing a crowd or hosting a lively social event[44]. It may mean merely that they will have to make a bit more of an effort than a natural extravert would in such circumstances; and this is likely to be a problem only if they are going to have to do a great deal of such things under pressure, so that they don't get an opportunity to recharge their batteries. Busy managers on a selection panel, untrained in using tests, are unlikely to give this important distinction the weight it deserves.

Moreover, how easy is it for assessors to judge whether a particular job calls for extraverted behaviour anyway? Many jobs can be performed in very different ways, as is clear from the fact that there is a perennial debate about whether leadership styles are important (see Chapter 8 below). People often have a lot of scope to mould their

---

Government study commented (p 95) "The evidence…raises questions about the validity of the MBTI…Nor has the instrument been validated in a long-term study of successful and unsuccessful careers. Lacking such evidence, it is a curiosity why the instrument is used so widely, particularly in large organizations." More recently see Petersen V C, 2006, *MBTI – Distorted reflections of personality?*, Working Paper, Aarhus School of Business. Some other later work has been rather less critical, but assessment of such findings remains difficult because so many people working in the area have some kind of financial interest in the use of psychometric tests.

[44] The idea of absolute and unchangeable character traits was exploded in the 1980s, though some conservative psychologists continue to resist it (see Roberts B W & DelVecchio W F, 2000, "The rank-order consistency of personality from childhood to old age: A quantitative review of longitudinal studies", *Psychological Bulletin*, vol 126 pp 3-25).

work role to their own preferred way of behaving, and this is more so the more complex or senior a job is. It is sometimes argued that managers need to be extraverts, since "they have to relate to other people"[45]; yet this is misleading, since introverts relate to others too, and can in any event produce extraverted behaviour if they need to[46].

Compare the example of stage actors. They perform in public to large audiences, and one would think that they more than anyone would need to be extraverts; yet the greatest comics, such as Tony Hancock or Kenneth Williams, have been haunted by depression (an introverted characteristic), and to all appearances have drawn the energy and edginess of their professional success from the conflict between their stage persona and their inner self. In any event, population studies tend to show that most people who score well on intelligence are on balance introverts[47]; and that does not mean that all of them are bad at their jobs.

Anyway, people adapt: they bed into their role. Not only do they often mould the job around themselves, focusing on those aspects which they do best. There is evidence that one's social context (at home or at work) influences one's score on personality tests. That implies that, whatever one's underlying preferences, if one is called on to behave a lot in a certain way, then one develops a greater ease and comfort with behaving like that. This is one reason why the test-retest consistency of personality

---

[45] Stewart R, 1988, *Managers and their jobs*, Macmillan, London; Bartram D, 1992, "The personality of UK managers: 16PF norms for short-listed applicants", *Journal of Occupational and Organizational Psychology*, 65 pp 159-172.

[46] Attempts to show a link between extraversion and performance have only showed a weak relationship: Barrick M R, Mount M K and Judge T A, 2001, "Personality and performance at the beginning of the new millennium: what do we know and where do we go next?", *International Journal of Selection and Assessment*, 9 pp 9-30.

[47] Furnham A, Forde L and Cotter T, 1998, "Personality and intelligence", *Personality and Individual Differences*, 24:2, 187–192; Furnham A, Moutafi J & Paltiel L, 2005, "Intelligence in Relation to Jung's Personality Types", *Individual Differences Research*, 3(1) pp 2-13.

tests is not all that good: people do change over time, so what you get in a recruitment test may not reflect the results if you try again once the candidate has started work in the job.

Personality tests are self-reports, and results can also be faked. The test publishers have an obvious interest in being sceptical of this. And they do indeed do their best to set up ways of spotting distortions. But the truth is that they are not infallible. If the candidate has an idea what is being looked for, and is familiar with the test, it can be done[48].

Finally, those making selections seldom look at the numerical scores of personality tests: they look at the text reports, which these days are produced automatically by software. Such reports tend to be better at looking at the interactions between the measures overall, than at the subtlety of the strengths of the measures individually. For example, where someone is broadly in equal balance between introversion and extraversion, but scores just a little higher on the first, they will often give the false impression that s/he is no different from someone who comes out way up the introversion scale and with almost no extraversion score[49].

Hence personality tests, though they appear very much like respectable objective science, are often unreliable, are very hard to use, and may well measure things which have little relation to the probable work performance of a candidate, if appointed to the job.

A final point to be cautious about is that tests can produce different results from people of different sex, race

---

[48] Krahé B, 1989, "Faking personality profiles on a standard personality inventory", *Personality and Individual Differences*, vol 10 no 4, pp 437-443; Kleinmann M, Ingold P, Lievens F, Jansen A, Melchers K, & Konig C, 2011, "A different look at why selection procedures work: The role of candidates' ability to identify criteria", *Organizational Psychology Review*, vol 1 (2), pp 128-146.

[49] Some tests, referred to as "type" rather than "trait" tests, actually institutionalise this distortion in the design of the test in order to produce results that are easier to understand (the MBTI is one).

or social background. This is not a good thing if one is looking for the best candidate, and may land one before a tribunal accused of unfair discrimination. Trained test administrators will be alive to these issues: do not try to use tests without guidance.

Selection review and validation

Where recruitment of similar staff is likely to be continual (for example in a large call centre or some industrial settings) it will be worth validating the effectiveness and relevance of selection procedures by assessing the performance and retention of staff some period of time after their engagement. Such assessment is complex, since external factors such as changes in the labour market cannot be excluded, and professional help may be needed for it to be done well.

Selection for dismissal

The pool of skills in an organisation is of course not only affected by recruitment. It is also important, though more sensitive, to seek to remove people who turn out not to have the skills which the organisation needs, or to have once had them but lost them, or to have skills which are no longer needed as a result of changing circumstances. This will sometimes be in the course of inefficiency procedures, and sometimes in the course of redundancy exercises in lean times. In both cases, practice will be confined by employment relations considerations and legal constraints. In principle, methods used in selection for redundancy can mirror those in selection for recruitment, but legal provisions and natural justice demand that they be exercised in a more fully accountable way and with even greater attention to the use of objective evidence in the decision.

Selection for promotion raises very similar issues to selection for recruitment. But there are some differences.

In part, these are simply down to the fact that the people involved are already part of the organisation. Their strengths and weaknesses ought to be known, and one of the key needs is to ensure that that knowledge can be used in the promotion decision in a way which is effective, and which is seen to be equitable by them and others. Line management systems need to be able to generate the necessary information for this, for example written annual reports with sections on promotability. This helps to anchor decisions and to avoid too much reliance on gossip and personal contacts, or treating newer staff too differently from those who have been in place for many years.

Selection for promotion

People are sometimes selected for their potential, whether as part of selection for immediate promotion or to feed a development programme (a classic UK example is "fast stream" recruits earmarked for accelerated promotion, say in the civil service or in large firms like Shell). Such schemes, which worked well in the stability of the post-war consensus, have come under strain in recent years as a result of growing political, economic and commercial volatilities, and there is also an increasingly active debate about what constitutes "potential"[50].

Potential

Generally, this is seen as either the ability to take on effectively a broader scope and senior (or in time top leadership) roles, or else the ability to perform well in areas key to the organisation's strategic objectives; and people with potential can be seen as grouped in particular disciplinary talent pools (eg finance, engineering, HR). However, predicting future abilities is little easier for a business leader, or for a psychologist, than for a punter in a horse race. And it does not help that precise definitions of "potential" are seldom made explicit, and often vary widely within an organisation. It is likely that past success in

---

[50] See Silzer R and Church A H, "Pearls and perils of identifying potential", *Industrial and Organizational Psychology*, 2009 vol 2 no 4 pp 377-412.

learning, and interest in and openness to future learning, are the only criteria which have much chance of identifying people with "potential". Nevertheless, relying simply on the standard of current performance is unlikely to be in itself a good way of making promotion decisions.

The Peter Prin- ciple

Other issues may affect promotion. In 1968 the British reading public, already excited by *Parkinson's Law*[51] which had been published a few years before and was still in the shops, discovered a new book on the shelves with a similar sort of title: *The Peter Principle*, written by an American academic, Dr Laurence Peter[52]. This argued that in a hierarchy every employee tends to rise to his level of incompetence. Thus people who are particularly good at their work get promoted until they reach a level where they are no longer so; thereafter, they are passengers in the organisation, and the work has to be done by those employees who have not yet reached their level of incompetence.

The message was half-humorous, and is such a challenge to conventional wisdom that nobody seems to have been quite sure what to do with it. Evidently there was some underlying truth in it somewhere, and it found its way into the curriculum of a number of US management courses. Observation and assertion were the basis of the original book, though a study in 2000 suggested that there might be statistical reasons to explain it as inevitable[53]. In 2009 systematic simulations of promotion dynamics were carried

---

[51] "Work expands so as to fill the time available for its completion": Parkinson C N, 2002, *Parkinson's Law: or the Pursuit of Progress*, Penguin Modern Classics, Harmondsworth.

[52] Peter L J and Hull R, 1971, *The Peter Principle: why things always go wrong*, Pan Books, London.

[53] Lazear E P, 2000, *The Peter Principle: Promotions and Declining Productivity*: http://www-siepr.stanford.edu/Papers/pdf/00-04.pdf; see also Pluchino A, Rapisarda A and Garofalo C, 2011, *Efficient Promotion Strategies in Hierarchical Organiza- tions*, Physica A, pp 3496-3511.

out, and renewed the challenge by proposing that promotion on a random basis might actually be more successful than the elaborate procedures which are often followed[54].

Random promotions would stand conventional wisdom on its head. They would obviously be seen as deeply unfair, and have no chance of being widely adopted. Commentators have suggested rather desperately that rotating people between jobs, which is a bit more recognisable as a practice, would achieve some of the benefits and minimise the risks caused by promotions on the Peter Principle[55]. It is perhaps worth recalling that the ancient Athenians appointed citizens to a number of important public offices by lot rather than on apparent merit, and the fact that they went on doing it for generations suggests that it cannot have been a total disaster[56].

Ultimately, what you think of the Peter Principle is up to you. If, like most people, you opt for a more considered approach, you do have one reassuring thing to fall back on: in seeking to get enough and not too many people with the right skills you'll have a lot of support from robust scientific research into the right techniques to use.

---

[54] Pluchino A, Rapisarda A, Garofalo C, 2010, "The Peter Principle Revisited: A Computational Study": *Physica* A 389 (2010) 467.

[55] Rajiv Mehta of the New Jersey Institute of Technology, quoted by Mark Buchanan in *New Scientist*, 19 December 2009 p 69.

[56] Google has tried it too, reputedly with reasonable results: BBC R4, *Analysis*, "Do Leaders make a Difference?", broadcast 7 November 2011, edited by Innes Bowen.

Chapter 3: Skills

This chapter discusses whether an organisation can just recruit the staff it needs or has to train them. It warns of the dangers of subjectivity and not being clear about what is needed. It describes the learning cycle and discusses learning styles. It looks at different kinds of training, and the problems of management training in particular, and addresses how learning transfers to the workplace, and how training can be evaluated.

"I don't think that in my lifetime there will be a woman Prime Minister."
Mrs Margaret Thatcher, 5 March 1973:
BBC interview by Valerie Singleton and others

Key message of this chapter: skill acquisition is well understood. Not everyone can acquire all skills, but mistakes in imparting them can be avoided.

We get the skills needed in an organisation either by getting the right people into or out of it, as described in the last chapter, or by training and educating the people there already.

Hard-to-acquire skills general

Some skills people can only acquire with a struggle, and this may mean it is much easier to recruit new staff who have them already, than to try to make existing staff skilled in them through training. For example, research has found that creativity may well be stimulated by living in a foreign country[57]. Of course, creativity must have many sources and stimuli, not just this one. But it does suggest that, from this perspective at least, firms without overseas offices are more likely to get people with that skill by recruiting for it, than by trying to train it into them.

---

[57] Maddux W W and Galinsky A D, "Cultural Borders and Mental Barriers: The Relationship Between Living Abroad and Creativity", *Journal of Personality and Social Psychology* 2009, vol 96 no 5, pp 1047–1061. This research did not address what aspect of living in a foreign country contributed to creativity (it's easy to make guesses - perhaps it is a situation where you have to improvise a lot, faced with urgent practical problems?). But it did suggest that, while some aspects of creativity were merely improved in people who had lived abroad, other aspects, which occurred among those who had, were not seen at all among those who had not.

In many circumstances, however, if skills are needed, it often makes sense to train. There are of course costs, but they are generally the costs of getting the process right, while with recruitment, as we have seen, a lot of effort is often wasted. And training has been demonstrated to be one of the most effective interventions to improve performance[58]. *Failure to train*

Training, however, is an activity on which Britain has for generations had an absurdly poor record, and over which a long succession of governments have wrung their hands. Despite years of attention to this, even in 1990 only 40% of employers had a training budget – which is to say, of course, that more than half did not[59]. Indeed, in some ways our record has got even worse over the years: apprenticeships once meant that many industrial workers, at least, got decent initial training, but the days are now long gone when a study of forty-seven British firms found only three which took no apprentices[60]. The current situation is at least as bad as it ever was[61].

Why organisations in Britain find it so hard to train people is a bit of a mystery, especially when there isn't a long tradition of high-level training in secondary or tertiary education to make up for it, as there is in, say, Germany (it's only in the last generation that it's become common here for engineers, surveyors, accountants, solicitors or nurses to study the profession at university, rather than practically, on the job, with the help of evening classes or day-release). Where, after all, do employers expect skills to come from?

---

[58] Guzzo R A , Jette R D and Katzell R A, 1985, "The effects of psychologically based intervention programs on worker productivity: a meta-analysis", *Personnel Psychology*, vol 38, pp 275-91

[59] Incomes Data Services (1990) *Training Strategies*, Study No. 460.

[60] Gater A, Insull D, Lind H and Seglow P, 1966, *Attitudes in British Management: a P.E.P. Report*, Penguin Press, Harmondsworth, p 94 [PEP was an early think-tank called Political and Economic Planning].

[61] Musset P and Field S, 2013, *A Skills Beyond School Review of England*, OECD Reviews of Vocational Education and Training, OECD, Paris.

Back in the 1970s the tripartite National Economic Development Council held some bad-tempered debates on the matter. These sounded a bit like the Monty Python sketch of the Three Social Classes. The government said that, as the benefit would go to businesses and employees, these should pay. Employers complained that, if they paid, trained staff would just be poached by firms that didn't meet training costs, and that therefore if it was in the public interest the government should pay – or maybe the employees. The unions said the workers couldn't afford it.

Sometimes one feels that things have hardly moved on from that impasse; and recent OECD work shows all categories of Britons scoring relatively poorly on literacy and numeracy, and all save those with degrees scoring badly on problem-solving in a technological world as well[62]. Today's studies, though, do suggest a slightly different emphasis from that of the 1970s – namely, that now there is a new problem as well, short-termism imposed by the financial institutions, since training is something with longer-term returns that tends to get squeezed out of the budget in order to meet quarterly shareholder targets[63].

Training down to employers

The solution, unwelcome to some, is perhaps suggested by a 1991 study of quality production methods. That noted that British managers are appraised on taking responsibility and meeting financial and production targets, not on how well they are developing their staff; and that practice is quite different in good Japanese companies[64]. It seems inescapable that British firms should meet the costs if they want the

---

[62] eg http://gpseducation.oecd.org/CountryProfile?primaryCountry=UKM&treshold=10&topic=AS [accessed October 2013].

[63] Legge K, 2005, *Human Resource Management: rhetoric and realities*, pp 273-274, Palgrave Macmillan, Basingstoke. There is a brief but helpful discussion of issues such as training which bear on the social responsibility of commercial businesses at Kay J, 1993, *Foundations of Corporate Success*, pp 324-326, OUP, Oxford.

[64] Storey J, Okazaki-Ward L, Edwards P K, Gow I and Sisson K, 1991, "Management Careers and Management Development: a comparative analysis of Britain and Japan", *Human Resource Management Journal*, vol 1(3) pp 33-57.

skills; and that, as Japan has shown, the cost of training and development can be greatly reduced if these are properly planned, and integrated into the work processes (besides, poor skills lead to a lot of hidden costs in recruitment, which are seldom taken into account in comparisons). The moral is clear. Skills need to be paid for like all other resources: if firms need them they must stop thinking they will appear by magic, and find the time and money to provide training – moreover, if they pay attention and do it cleverly, they can still keep costs to a minimum.

There are other advantages when training is sponsored by the employer. He who pays the piper calls the tune, and an employer commissioning training ought to get precisely the training he needs[65]. Again, acquiring new skills is a risky business. Trainees are often unsure whether they will succeed or fail, and this will cause anxiety, especially if they are being trained within the organisation or alongside colleagues who may report back on them. Hence an important part of training and development is encouraging the confidence of the trainee[66]; this needs the commitment of the line manager as well as training staff.

Who pays can also distort the effectiveness of training. Large organisations, for example in the armed services, which used to fund recruits for general qualifications in technical trades, have sometimes now been encouraged by financial pressures to restrict training to the specific skills only which will be needed on the next project; this diminishes overall workforce skills, and is likely to reduce the sense of autonomy, commitment and performance of employees.

---

[65] See Musset P and Field S, 2013, *A Skills Beyond School Review of England*, OECD Reviews of Vocational Education and Training, OECD, Paris.
[66] Bandura A, 1977, "Self-efficacy: towards a unifying theory of behavioural change", *Psychological Review*, vol 84 no 2, pp 191-215.

Various kinds of training are needed in organisations. Some training needs to be given on the sheep-dip principle to everyone (such as fire drills, or changes to health and safety rules); some needs to be given to particular divisions or grades (such as technical developments, or changes to employment law). And some is required by individuals, either to improve their performance in their current jobs or to prepare them for future roles. Planning is needed to ensure that the right training goes to the right people at the right time.

Kinds of training

The actual process of training is much studied and well understood. Good trainers will pay attention in training design to issues of consistency and repetition, variation to maintain interest, explanation of principles as well as training content, breaking down of complex tasks into their components, timing and specificity of feedback, and the need to train to a somewhat higher level of skill than is likely to be required in routine practice, as well as to handling well the emotional context, for example in relation to the confidence of trainees and the supportiveness of the learning group.

Manage-ment training

Management training sometimes seems especially poor, and this is not new. A speaker in Parliament in 1947 remarked "It is still a widely-held belief that to set up in business it is sufficient to have a little practical experience and some natural aptitude."[67]. Even by the 1960s, the MD of one large shipbuilding firm observed expansively, "I think I'm more successful in training my own managers. Getting intelligent people and then training them in [this firm's] policies is the most successful way"; at another shipbuilders' they commented, "We haven't been successful [with management training] because of the inertia and resistance to anything non-traditional". And at a booming

---

[67] Lord Chorley on the Industrial Organisation Bill, *Hansard*, HL 18 June 1947 vol 148 col 956.

large manufacturing firm the MD said, "...we felt that we ought to be able to train most decent people up within our own organisation by shunting them around and ... starting to give the chap [*sic*] a chance to develop within the company, so we have not used outside courses to any extent."[68]

Whether things have changed very much since then is an interesting question, though I think there is a much wider perception that ambitious people are especially hungry for training early in their careers; we shall come back to leadership issues in a later chapter. But I should note at this point that, in the important area of first-line managers, a thorough and recent cross-sectoral study has found that the availability of training, both in technical matters and in soft leadership skills, has a huge impact on both the commitment and the job satisfaction of supervisors[69].

One study also suggests that being in a job that you have opted to be in is linked, through motivation, to positive training outcomes. The authors conclude "it is important, whenever possible, to grant employees their choice of job when being moved within an organization" – not just for the sake of long-term aspirations, or their immediate perform-ance, but in terms of their capacity and willingness to improve over time[70].

---

[68] Gater A, Insull D, Lind H and Seglow P, 1966, *Attitudes in British Management: a P.E.P. Report*, Penguin Press, Harmondsworth, p 51.
[69] Purcell J, Kinnie N, Hutchinson S, Rayton B and Swart J, 2003, *Understanding the People and Performance Link: unlocking the black box*, CIPD London, pp 67-68.
[70] Patrick J, Smy V, Tombs M, & Shelton K, 2012, "Being in one's chosen job determines pre-training attitudes and training outcomes", *Journal of Occupational and Organizational Psychology*, 85 (2), 245-25.

How people learn

Human capacities for acquiring new skills have their limits, and a good deal is known about what these are[71]. This enables robust training programmes to be designed for enabling people to perform complex and demanding tasks, such as flying aircraft or controlling nuclear reactors. Nevertheless, it is clear that some people seem to respond to certain methods of training better than others, and this has given rise to a continuing debate over how people can be best identified for different kinds of training and development.

One learns by reflecting on experience (sometimes the experience of one's own actions, and sometimes the experience of being taught). Then one acts on the understanding one has gained, and observes what happens, and reflects again on the results. The idea that one builds one's knowledge and skills through such a cyclical process goes back at least to Aristotle. But in the context of work skills this long-standing model was crystallised helpfully by David Kolb of Ohio in the 1970s[72]. This sees people going through repeated cycles of the following stages:

- concrete experience,
- observation of and reflection on that experience,
- formation of abstract concepts based upon the reflection,
- testing the new concepts in practice

Learning styles

Kolb took this idea further by proposing that individuals differ in their effectiveness in or comfortableness with these four stages, and that psychometric tests could identify from this which of four learning styles they exhibit; to these he gave the rather opaque names of "converger", "diverger", "assimilator", and "accommodator".

---

[71] Howell W C and Cooke N J, 1989, "Training the human information processor: A review of cognitive models.", in Goldstein I L, *Training and development in organizations*, Jossey-Bass, San Francisco, CA, US, pp 121-182.
[72] Kolb D A and Fry R, 1975, "Toward an applied theory of experiential learning". in Cooper C (*ed.*), *Theories of Group Process*, John Wiley, London.

A quite different and rather more concrete idea of learning styles also came forward at a similar time. The approach known as neuro-linguistic programming (NLP) was developed in the 1960s within the human potential movement as part of New Age thinking, and gave rise to a theory that individuals have sensory preferences in how they get and give out information, classifying these into four channels: visual, auditory, reading/writing and kinaesthetic[73]. NLP practitioners in training and development argued that analysis of such preferences would help to assign trainees more effectively to different modes of learning (book study, training course &c).

Though it has achieved a certain foothold in the HR community, NLP is highly controversial, and has been described as pseudo-science[74].

More broadly, the whole idea of learning styles, however plausible it may sound, has been condemned as lacking any effective evidence in its favour[75]. It is probably

---

[73] See now Fleming N D & Mills C, 1992, "Not Another Inventory, Rather a Catalyst for Reflection", *To Improve the Academy*, 11, 137-155.

[74] e.g. Witkowski T, 2010, "Thirty-Five Years of Research on Neuro-Linguistic Programming. NLP Research Data Base. State of the Art or Pseudoscientific Decoration?", *Polish Psychological Bulletin*, vol 41 (2) pp 58-66; Devilly G J, 2005, "Power therapies and possible threats to the science of psychology and psychiatry". *Australian and New Zealand Journal of Psychiatry*, vol 39 (6) pp 437-45. One authority remarks "NLP is a thoroughly fake title, designed to give the impression of scientific respectability. NLP has little to do with neurology, linguistics, or even the respectable sub-discipline of neurolinguistics" (Corballis M C, 1999, "Are we in our right minds?" in Della Sala S (*ed.*), *Mind myths* (pp. 26-42). Wiley, Chichester).

[75] This debate carries more emotional charge than most in the management field, probably because it applies not just to training for adults who can take responsibility for themselves, but also to the education of children who are more vulnerable. Evidence is reviewed at Coffield F, Moseley D, Hall E and Ecclestone K, 2004, *Learning styles and pedagogy in post-16 learning: a systematic and critical review*, London, Learning and Skills Network; Hargreaves D (*chair*), 2005, *About Learning: Report of the Learning Working Group*, London, Demos, page 11 (available by download from http://www.demos.co.uk/publications/aboutlearning); Pashler H, McDaniel M, Rohrer D, Bjork R, 2008, "Learning styles: Concepts and evidence", *Psychological Science in the Public Interest* 9, pp. 105-119.

not worth spending money on. If you want to acquire new skills, though, or you want your staff to do so, there will usually be a choice of methods, and of course there are differences between the merits of these. The decision between them will depend mainly on three things: cost, effectiveness and social factors.

Cost is fairly straightforward, varying mainly with the number of learners involved, any need for travel, and the quality of the teachers and institutions.

Effectiveness will also depend on the latter quality. It will also depend on whether what is to be acquired is information or skills: skills need embedding through active repetition[76] and more help from the discipline of social interaction.

Other social factors are often extrinsic to the strict skills agenda, but may be helpful in other ways. Will a course enable the trainee to form useful social or networking connections with people in other parts of the organisation or the industry? Is a training course away from home seen as a "jolly", or perhaps as essential career development, in either case forming, in effect, a part of the employee's reward package? Will they get a tablet device for it at the employer's expense? Will it involve going to a prestigious college about which they can boast, or which will look good on their cv?

Coaching

Where the need is to improve skills rather than to impart knowledge, coaching has in recent years become a popular, indeed fashionable, route to work-related learning. The coaching discipline has rapidly grown, developing professional associations, and distinctions between different kinds

---

[76] Bloom B S, 1984, "The 2 Sigma Problem: The Search for Methods of Group Instruction as Effective as One-to-One Tutoring", *Educational Researcher* vol 13, No. 6, pp. 4-16.

of coaching[77]. It involves one-to-one support for learners, so it is expensive, and one might therefore think that its success was driven by marketing hype from the bandwagon of coaching firms which has suddenly sprung up – and this creates a climate which will of course influence even academic papers, however scrupulous the peer-review process. Moreover, the quality of what is offered, both by line managers and by professional coaches, can vary greatly. In addition, it is difficult to find hard evidence comparing its effectiveness and efficiency with other ways of delivering better skills.

However, there are good *a priori* reasons why a one-to-one approach might work well. It is established that we respond best to prompt feedback, and coaching can offer this; coaching is automatically tailored to an individual's needs; it is easier to persuade people to be coached than to go on courses; a good coach will provide better challenge as well as information, not just offering new skills but delving deeper to correct unsatisfactory skillsets; coaching tends to be tailored to practical problems, bringing theory down to earth; a coach, unlike a training course leader, can stay around to supervise the transfer of new skills to the workplace. You might compare the tutorial system at Oxbridge, which has certainly stood the test of time.

Unfortunately it is very difficult to evaluate coaching. There is no shortage of articles (often by coaches) reporting enthusiastic feedback from people coached. But serious analysis is rare. Even the basic credibility of coaching has been questioned, with a recent meta-analysis[78] finding that, if you ask about its effectiveness, people coached will respond saying that their performance had improved by

---

[77] These remarks are not intended to address so-called "life coaching", which can shade into psychotherapy; cp Beltrán R, 2012, *Pensar el Negocio*, Buenos Aires, pp 289-292.

[78] A meta-analysis is a method of combining a number of different studies in order to dilute technical weaknesses and increase statistical reliability.

about 25%, while their colleagues will say that it had actually fallen off, sometimes by up to 50%[79]. And more traditional studies do not do much better.

Employers are very poor at assessing coaching[80], and results are so inconsistent as to be, to say the least, suspect. One fairly sophisticated US study found return on investment of well over 2000%[81], another 200%[82]; both the magnitude and the diversity of these figures suggest serious methodological problems, and it is no surprise that a more thoughtful survey has concluded "data from such studies are at the level of collective anecdote"[83].

There are formal reasons why evaluation is difficult: since coaching focuses so much on the individual, the classic scientific pre-post study with a control group is not practical. But one also needs to bear in mind that there are poor reasons as well as good ones for going for coaching. The person coached gets the ego-massaging experience of

---

[79] De Meusea K P, Daia G & Leeb R J, 2009, "Evaluating the effectiveness of executive coaching: beyond ROI?", *Coaching: An International Journal of Theory, Research and Practice*, Volume 2, Issue 2, pages 117-134.

[80] CIPD, 2011, *The Coaching Climate: survey report*. CIPD, pp 7-8.

[81] Bernard P, 2006, *ROI and Coaching: Applying Metrics to Measure the Effectiveness of Coaching Programs*, Paul Bernard Associates: pdf at www. paulbernard.net/articles/Sample_ROI_study.pdf [accessed 9 November 2012]: there is a major weakness in its approach, an assumption that all performance improvement in the period is caused by the coaching alone – though this must be seen in the light of very high ROIs rising to 52,000%. See also the studies cited in De Meusea 2009 ranging between 470% and 790% ROI, figures which the author generously describes as "tenuous".

[82] Anderson M, 2001, *"Case study on the return on investment of executive coaching"*, Executive briefing, Metrix Global, Des Moines, USA: available at http://www.coachfederation.org/includes/docs/053metrixglobal-coaching-roi-briefing .pdf [accessed 10 November 2012]. Quantification of the benefits in this study was by subjective judgement by the beneficiaries.

[83] MacKie D, 2007, "Evaluating the effectiveness of executive coaching: Where are we now and where do we need to be?". *Australian Psychologist*, 42: 310–318. An example is Parker-Wilkins V, 2006, "The business impact of executive coaching: demonstrating monetary value", *Industrial and Commercial Training*, vol 38 issue 3 pp 122-127: the method here was to ask 28 volunteers (ie a small and non-random sample) in one US company each to estimate the benefits they had got from coaching, their monetary value, and how confident they were in their estimates; and then proudly to claim a 700% ROI.

personal attention. Colleagues and bosses are not incon-
venienced by him or her going off for training at a busy
time. HR gets to set up training without the administrative
hassle of having to get a dozen busy people together at the
same time for a course. The coach gets a good fee, and work
that generally needs less elaborate planning than a more
formal programme.

Hence it is taking a while for the evaluation of coaching
as a way of gaining skills to shake down. That is not a good
reason to avoid coaching altogether: it has significant
attractions, even if its benefits are not yet as robustly
identified as they might be. However, it is a warning not to
regard it as a panacea.

And there are some guidelines it is worth following. To
be effective a coaching intervention should not be open-
ended: organisational data needs to be used to align it with
business goals[84]. It is important that clear objectives are set
for a coaching programme before it is embarked on, and
progress against them monitored. Once coaching begins, it
is often found that the apparent problem is not the real one
and that the direction of travel needs to be changed, so the
objectives need frequent formal reviews at the early stages.
Personal chemistry between the coach and their executive
can be important, and people need to understand that the
coach can be changed if it is not working. There needs from
the start to be an evaluation plan. If these guidelines are
used, then coaching will have its place in a skills development or CPD programme.

More recent than coaching are the opportunities that
new technology offers for skills development. People have
always sought advice from colleagues about their work,
especially within the professions, and the web has much

---

[84] CIPD, 2012, *Coaching: the evidence base*, CIPD, pp 8-10; this is contrary to early
coaching approaches which were influenced by psychotherapy ethics and saw coaching by definition as private and confidential.

increased the opportunities for this on sites from Twitter to those of professional institutions. Video clips can be developed to be shown to staff just before they undertake tasks, so they can perform them with a model fresh in their minds. Data analysis of performance reports can also be used to identify training opportunities[85].

Formally programmed education is now available on-line very cost-effectively, at a basic level through websites such as Khan Academy, and at a higher one through networks such as Futurelearn, EdX, Coursera and Udacity. They clearly offer a huge opportunity for wider access to teaching excellence[86]. The efficacy of new technology approaches has not been effectively analysed. It is notable that they have suffered in the past from a weakness in social support to the learning process. They more recently claim to have overcome this, but there is as yet little firm evidence either way.

Barriers to learn-ing
There is a tendency for employees and their line managers to struggle somewhat to get training set up: those affected often have to be persuaded to accept the need for training, a suitable course has to be identified, money has to be found to pay for it, the time of the employee has to be freed up for the training activity, and cover often needs to be put in place so that the work gets done in their absence. This often leaves people rather sitting back once the course has begun, with an assumption that the effort is now over, and that the new skills and knowledge will follow automatically. Unfortunately this is not the case: though the trainers have a job to do, training is unlikely to produce real

[85] Bird J, 2013, "Technology means wisdom is shared on demand", *Financial Times*, 6 November 2013.
[86] Means B *et al.*, 2010, *Evaluation of Evidence-Based Practices in Online Learning: A Meta-Analysis and Review of Online Learning Studies*, US Department of Education, Washington DC.

improvement without further input both by the trainee and by their line manager.

Thus a lot of effort goes into training. But less goes into whether it works, and a lot of organisational psychologists' effort has rightly gone into this issue. Two things are particularly important: (i) evaluation, both of whether a particular training course is generally effective, and of whether it has brought about change in a particular trainee, and (ii) whether skills imparted in the safe context of the training course actually survive into real life in the workplace[87].

A robust model of evaluation was developed in the 1960s by Donald Kirkpatrick of Wisconsin in the USA, and is still the gold standard for such examination. It assesses training at four levels: *Training evaluation*

> the reaction of the trainee to the training

> the increase in knowledge or skills resulting from the training

> the change in behaviour on the job and improvement in job performance of the trainee

> the results of the training on business outcomes[88].

This model has been found successful and is still widely followed. But it is not always all that easy to use. For example, even when the question someone is asked is how much they learned on a course, then if they enjoyed it, even if they learned nothing, they are fairly likely to score it highly. And if someone gets trained in a skill which is important but which they only expect to use occasionally (such as emergency response, or maybe media interview technique) then assessing the effect of the training on business outcomes, or often even of their job performance

---

[87] One US study found that only 10% of training spend actually resulted in transfer to the job: Georgenson D L, 1982, "The problem of transfer calls for partnership", *Training and Development Journal*, vol 36(10) pp 75-78.

[88] Most recently in Kirkpatrick D L and Kirkpatrick J D, 2006, *Evaluating Training Programs*, Berrett-Koehler Publishers, San Francisco, USA.

overall, is not always easy, or even possible. Hence advice will usually be helpful.

Making sure that training actually transfers into real life is a slightly different problem. Good trainers will be able to build mechanisms into training to support such a transfer.

Appli-cation of training However, while evaluation may be left to training professionals, the transfer is always going to depend very much on the line manager. This will usually be the person who can ensure, after the training, that the trainee has the chance to embed their new skills by exercising them while they are still fresh, who can support them in their faltering steps on new ground so as to ensure that they do not lose their confidence, and who can make sure that new skills are reinforced and developed from time to time by appropriate in-service training[89].

A word about men and women, too. We all know that you're not allowed to discriminate against women in recruitment and promotion, but many of us have been told that women are better at "soft skills" or "communication" or "people skills", or men are better at difficult decisions. This may or may not be true as a generalisation. What is certainly true is that it is not a biological difference between men and women, and that many men are better than many women at some of the things they are supposed to be worse at, and *vice versa*[90]. So don't stereotype, or you may make the wrong decisions.

Thus people with the right skills are essential for all organisations. Whether we recruit them, or train them, we can look to pretty good expert advice on how to do it well.

---

[89] Baldwin T T and Ford J K, 1988, "Transfer of Training: a review and directions for further research", *Personnel Psychology*, 41, pp 63-105.
[90] Fine C, 2011, *Delusions of Gender: the real science behind sex differences*, Icon Books, London.

However, even if we do it well, we should reconcile ourselves to the fact that a proportion of our decisions about this will go wrong.

Whether people's skills are good or just adequate, the effectiveness of their contribution to the organisation depends on whether they choose to use them or not. This will generally depend on how engaged they are with their jobs.

Chapter 4: Engagement

This chapter looks at the relationship between engagement and performance, and whether this varies for different groups of staff. It goes on to discuss the impact of the formal contract (including pay and job security) and the informal or "psychological" contract (including trust, the sense of whether a job is worthwhile, and feeling appreciated). It addresses stress, the freedom people have to decide on how they do their work, and the key role of targets. It touches on the effectiveness of contracting out.

"Anyone who has ever read a Dilbert strip knows that cynicism and passivity are endemic in large organisations. Only an ostrich could have missed that."

Gary Hamel, 2012

"The salary of the chief executive of the large corporation is not a market reward for achievement. It is frequently in the nature of a warm personal gesture by the individual to himself."

J K Galbraith, 1974

Key message of this chapter: Motivating people is tricky. Setting goals is established as an effective motivator; there has been recent progress with issues of trust and stress; money can be a great deceiver.

No organisation is effective unless its people care about what they are doing[91]. A very big international survey in 2007 suggested that only about 20% of people globally (14% in the UK) were fully engaged with their work, and that around 40% (44% in the UK) were distinctly disengaged[92].

---

[91] This is seen as a truism today, but has not always been so: one of the most authoritative experts on management has said "An employer has no business with a man's personality. Employment is a specific contract calling for specific performance and for nothing else. Any attempt of an employer to go beyond this is usurpation. It is immoral as well as illegal intrusion of privacy. It is abuse of power. An employee owes no "loyalty"…and no "attitudes" – he owes performance and nothing else…" Drucker P, 1973, *Management: Tasks, Responsibilities and Practices*, Harper and Row, New York, pp 424-5. But this behaviourist interpretation was effectively being demolished by experimental psychology at about the time that Drucker was writing.

[92] Towers Perrin, 2008, *Global Workforce Study 2007-2008*, Towers Perrin, New York, esp. pp 4 & 27. Note that I use the term "engagement" broadly in this chapter:

The British Government commissioned a major study in 2008 of how organisations could enhance their performance through employee engagement[93]. That study made a large collection of evidence that there is a connection between, on the one hand, employee engagement, and, on the other, in the private sector better financial performance, and in the public sector better outcomes. However, the evidence gathered was unspecific. It does not amount to proof.

Engagement: general

Yet it is common sense that any organisation needs to have a clear idea of how committed its people are; and many carry out regular engagement surveys with this in mind. Some, rather sluggishly, do little more about it than carry out the survey – and managers do need to remember that measurement is not a substitute for action[94].

To some extent engagement is not in the gift of an organisation's managers. The public mood follows fashion. Public trust in business has varied a great deal since 2001 in the United States, though rather less in Europe[95], and this must influence the attitudes of people in organisations on both sides of the Atlantic. Nevertheless, their feelings of engagement must depend far more on their own interactions at work.

---

in the academic literature there have been numerous attempts to refine it (see Macey W H, Schneider B, Barbera K M, and Young S A, 2009, *Employee Engagement: Tools for Analysis, Practice, and Competitive Advantage*, Wiley-Blackwell, West Sussex).

[93] MacLeod D and Clarke N, 2009, *Engaging for Success: enhancing performance through employee engagement: a report to Government*, Department for Business, Innovation and Skills, London.

[94] In February 2013 a research firm called Opinium found, from a study of 2,000 organisations in the UK carrying out engagement surveys, that most of them were top-down exercises, and tended to reinforce rather than challenge the notion that the views and feelings of employees were not valued by top management (http://www.lansons.com/pdfs/lansons-change-and-employee-engagement-event-report-final.pdf).

[95] The Edelman Company, 2009, *Edelman Trust Barometer 2009: the tenth global opinion leaders study*, The Edelman Company, Chicago, p 5.

Fair-
ness
How people see the fairness of their relationship with their employer is fundamental to their sense of engagement. Their terms of employment are a major part of this, including reward, of which pay is probably the most important part.

Pay is one of the most contentious areas in the field of motivation. Clearly, people will often try harder if told it will bring them more pay. But the consistency and even the effect of this is not straightforward, with measuring people's input and social consequences being common problems (even psychologists may be of less help here than in other areas, as like many employers they have a tendency to think in terms of individuals rather than teams). There is agreement, for example, that when people think they are being paid less than others who are making a similar or lesser contribution to the organisation, then they become resentful, dissatisfied and disengaged, and their performance often falls off[96]. But most other views about pay are contested. We shall look at pay again towards the end of this chapter.

Job
defin-
ition
After pay, the definition of the job is one of the most important formal components of the employment contract. Its importance is under-rated: poor job definition can lead to stressful over- or under-loading, or to fatal misunderstandings about someone's duties or performance. Always make sure that any post for which you are responsible is clearly defined.

But it is not just a matter of clarity: good job design will give workers a feeling that the job is worthwhile, a sense of responsibility for the work they are doing, and regular feed-

---

[96] Hence pay is generally seen as what is called a "hygiene factor", where paying too much has little effect, while paying too little has serious consequences: Hertzberg F, Mausner B and Snyderman B, 1959, *The Motivation to Work*, Wiley; Guzzo R A, Jette R D and Katzell R A, 1985, "The effects of psychologically based intervention programs on worker productivity: a meta-analysis", *Personnel Psychology*, 38, 275-91. An analogy in 2014 Britain might be a badger cull, where according to the Krebs report you can solve the badger problem in one place, only to find that this causes perturbation which only increases the problem round about.

back on how well they are doing it[97]. On the whole, even if the design is flawed, they will themselves, if they can, seek to improve its focus in this sense. And, whatever the precise description of a job, in most there still remains room for negotiation and flexibility. It used to be thought that senior managers had more flexibility than junior staff in setting the scope of their own roles. This now seems to be less the case[98], partly as a result of the accelerated pace of change affecting jobs today. The need for complex negotiation of job design highlights the importance of a good relationship between leaders and their team-members for this as for other aspects of management.

One of the key issues in job content is the degree of control which someone has over his work. Study after study has shown that the greater that is, the happier (and often the more productive) is the employee[99]. However, there is a dominant tradition of management styles, in line with Taylor's principles, where it is your boss rather than you who controls in detail what you do at work.

Control over one's work

Sometimes it is obvious that this is a bad idea. The Royal Navy in the late 19th century demanded unquestioning obedience to orders. In 1893 Vice-Admiral Sir George

---

[97] Hackman J R, 1991, "Work Design", in Steers R and Porter L (eds), *Motivation and Work Behaviour*, McGraw-Hill, pages 424-25.

[98] Berg J M *et al.*, "Perceiving and responding to challenges in job crafting at different ranks: when proactivity requires adaptivity", *Journal of Organizational Behavior*, 2010, vol. 31 no. 2-3, pp. 158-186; Hornung S *et al.*, "Beyond top-down and bottom-up work redesign: customizing job content through idiosyncratic deals", *Journal of Organizational Behavior*, 2010, vol. 31 no. 2-3, pp. 187-215. The Hornung study extended to Germany, so its findings are not solely applicable in the United States.

[99] Judge T A and Bono J E, 2000, "Relationship of core self-evaluations traits – self-esteem, generalized self-efficacy, locus of control, and emotional stability – with job satisfaction and job performance: a meta-analysis", *Journal of Applied Psychology*, vol 86(1), pp 80-92. The putative relationship between happiness and productivity has been hotly contested for many years (a special issue of the Journal of Organizational Behavior in January 1999 has a number of articles on the topic); it currently looks as if it depends on your definition of happiness.

Tryon, on exercise in the Levant, ordered the two parallel columns of the Mediterranean Fleet to turn inward when there was in fact not enough room for the manœuvre. His officers acted as instructed, and he died as his flagship HMS Victoria sank in the resultant collision[100].

Cultural issues can complicate the picture. Often, in societies without a tradition of much education, there is not much experience of junior staff having the skills needed to make the right decisions, and therefore less autonomy is tolerated.

But many managers are insecure and cling to too much control. It is true that more delegation requires more communication to see that things are co-ordinated; this can be expensive in staff time, and in an emergency it may not be practical at all. However, the importance of delegation or "subsidiarity" is increasingly recognised[101] (though middle-level jobs are also becoming hollowed out by automation, a tendency which is working at the same time in the opposite direction[102]).

This opens out one of the most important risks relating to job autonomy: the wide spread of the perception that managers speak the language of autonomy, while constantly making decisions which in practice exert detailed control[103]. Few errors are more effective than this kind of incongruity at demolishing the credibility of managers: it should be avoided at all costs.

Casual work   Another important part of terms of employment can be whether one has the relative security of a permanent

---

[100] Clowes W L, 1903, *The Royal Navy – A History from the Earliest Times to 1900*, London, vol 7 pp 415-426.

[101] e.g. Handy C, quoted in *Business Strategy Review*, London Business School 2010 Q2, p 88.

[102] Goos M *et al.*, "Job polarisation in Europe", *American Economic Review*, vol. 99(2), 2009, pp. 58–63; Davis G. F., "Job design meets organizational sociology", *Journal of Organizational Behavior*, 2010, vol 31 no 2-3, p 303.

[103] Wilmott H, 1993, "Strength is Ignorance; Slavery is Freedom: managing culture in modern organizations", *Journal of Management Studies*, vol 30 no 4, pp 515-552.

contract. The EU in the 1990s sought to extend the rights of workers on temporary or fixed-term contracts, suggesting that they were a disadvantaged group. Some research has suggested that this might be so only for low-skilled workers, while knowledge workers in high demand might be happy to maintain contract flexibility[104]. However, a substantial study in six countries has since indicated otherwise: in fact, *all* temporary workers reported more positive attitudes to their work than those with permanent contracts, and the lower skilled among these reported the highest levels of well-being[105]. Other evidence still points the other way[106], and the implications of this counter-intuitive finding are not yet clear.

But the formal terms of employment are by no means the only determinant of how people see the fairness of their relationship with their employer. Perhaps more so is what is known as the psychological contract. This term is used for the pattern of informal expectations which the employer has of the employee, and the employee of the employer, and of the obligations which match them[107]. Such expectations can be around control, such as whether a blind eye is turned if people leave after 3.30 pm on a Friday, provided they know they must stay late if there's an urgent job to finish. They

"Psycho-logical contract"

---

[104] O'Sullivan M, 1994, *Performance Effects of Fixed-term Contracts*, MSc dissertation, Birkbeck College, University of London; Marler J, Barringer M & Milkovich G, 2002, "Boundaryless and traditional contingent workers: worlds apart". *Journal of Organizational Behavior*, vol 23, pp 425-453.

[105] Guest D and Clinton M, 2006, *Temporary Employment Contracts, Workers' Well-Being and Behaviour: Evidence from the UK*, Department of Management Working Paper No. 38, King's College, London.

[106] e.g. Selenko E, Mäkikangas A, Mauno S, Kinnunen U, 2013, "How does job insecurity relate to self-reported job performance? Analysing curvilinear associations in a longitudinal sample", *Journal of Occupational & Organizational Psychology*, vol 86 no 4, pp 522-542.

[107] A recent authoritative definition is "the perceptions of both parties to the employment relationship, organisation and individual, of the reciprocal promises and obligations implied in that relationship": *Pressure at Work and the Psychological Contract*, 2002, Guest D E and Conway N, CIPD, London.

may be around status, such as the attitude to the use of taxis, or who gets a space in the office car park. They may be around development support, such as getting to conferences or training courses.

Union membership has declined, albeit reluctantly[108]. As a result, the direct relationship between an individual and his or her employer has become all the more important, and this throws the psychological contract into higher relief than ever.

Its key importance is that it is at the root of motivation at work. For most people, pay is not the main motivator of performance. In recent years big strides have been made in understanding what encourages people to deliver at work[109]. And it now looks very much as though what this is is a very fundamental principle in social psychology and social science, namely the idea of social exchange: that most people, if they get something from someone, even something non-material, feel under an obligation to give them something in return. Most relationships are established and supported by continued exchanges – whether of gifts or treats or money or prestige or praise, or other things, material or moral[110]. In organisations this seems to work as follows.

---

[108] Waddington J, 1992, "Trade union membership in Britain, 1980-1987: unemployment and restructuring", *British Journal of Industrial Relations*, 30, 287-324. Only about a quarter (27%) of UK employees are now union members, although union membership density is much higher in the public sector (57%) than the private sector (15%): Fulton L, 2011, *Worker representation in Europe*, Labour Research Department and ETUI (online publication). However, a fairly recent survey found that 75% of employees wanted legislation to introduce works councils: *Pressure at Work and the Psychological Contract*, 2002, Guest D E and Conway N, CIPD, London, p ix.

[109] Coyle-Shapiro J and Kessler I, 2000, "Consequences of the Psychological Contract for the Employment Relationship: a large scale survey", *Journal of Management Studies* 37 pp. 903-930; Purcell J, Kinnie N, Hutchinson S, Rayton B and Swart J, 2003, *Understanding the People and Performance Link: unlocking the black box*, CIPD London.

[110] Mauss M, 1950, *Essai sur le Don*, Presses Universitaires de France, Paris.

People see their organisation as represented by their managers. If their managers treat them in ways which meet or exceed their expectations, then they will feel more satisfied in their jobs and more committed to their organisation, engage more effectively with their tasks, and work more or better than at the basic level asked of them[111].

The way this works is complex and not fully understood, but we do know a range of things which employees may expect or hope that their employer will give them, and which can form an important component of the psychological contract. We shall come back to what they are in a moment.

But firstly, let's pause to think for a moment about trust, because trust is at the bottom of a lot of all this. One might think that, with the economic depression, trust has in general taken a battering recently. In fact, in both Europe and the USA trust in government, having hit a low point in 2007, had been gradually recovering until 2011, even though in 2012 it fell back again below 2008 levels; while trust in business, whose low point was in 2009, rose in 2010, then fell back in the following two years[112].

Trust

That is at a high level of generality. We have, however, a major recent study in the UK, covering 14 organisations from John Lewis to GKN to HMRC, which tells us a lot more[113]. Trust, like reputation, is hard to gain and easy to lose[114]. It is especially vulnerable in times of vigorous

---

[111] This is known as "discretionary behaviour" or "organisational citizenship behaviour".

[112] Edelman Trust Barometer 2012 [website http://trust.edelman.com/trust-download/global-results/]; "Europe" here means the UK, France and Germany. This is a very large survey of the informed public aged 35-64, using fairly unsophisticated questions.

[113] Hope-Hailey V, Searle R and Dietz G, 2012, *Where has all the trust gone?*, CIPD, Wimbledon; Gillespie N and Dietz G, 2009, "Trust repair after an organization-level failure" *Academy of Management Review* Vol 34, No 1, January. pp 127–145.

[114] O'Sullivan M, 1991, *Reputation in the Civil Service*, paper presented to Group for Anthropology in Policy and Practice conference on organisational anthropology at University College, Swansea.

change like the present, when managers are often confronted with dilemmas which seem capable of resolution only by betraying promises, especially promises to employees. Indeed, they may be so locked up in problems that they do not notice that they are eroding trust. So action should be taken to check, such as regular staff surveys and exit interviews. Rebuilding trust when it is broken is difficult, and requires not only system changes (such as new procedures) but also changes in behaviour by managers, including visible and consistent behaviour modelling by senior leaders. A good HR team can provide useful support (and a bad one can undermine the process)[115].

Trust in senior management is relatively low in the UK (especially in the public sector)[116], and trust in business generally is lower in the UK than in most other countries[117]. So business leaders in the UK need to work harder than their counterparts elsewhere to build and maintain trust. They need to be seen as competent, concerned for others, ethical and reasonably consistent. Truth, honesty, and not shooting the messenger when there is bad news, are the essential tools for this; and these skills are trainable. British culture is given to periphrasis and understatement, which may make this a challenge – but who is to say that it is more of a challenge than the impenetrable obfuscation of American business-speak?

Professionals and specialists are in a rather different situation from others. As has been shown, they tend to be relatively mobile, and they derive much of their satisfaction

---

[115] Hope-Hailey V, Searle R and Dietz G, 2012, *Where has all the trust gone?*, CIPD, Wimbledon; Gillespie N and Dietz G, 2009, "Trust repair after an organization-level failure" *Academy of Management Review* Vol 34, No 1, January. pp127–145.
[116] Hope-Hailey V &c, 2012, *Where has all the trust gone?*, CIPD, Wimbledon.
[117] Edelman Trust Barometer 2012; CIPD *Employee Outlook* surveys 2009-13. The British Social Attitudes survey similarly shows a decline in the belief that management 'is sincere in attempting to understand employees' views': **Bryson** A & **Forth J, 2010.** *The Evolution of the Modern Worker: Attitudes to Work*, NIESR Discussion Papers 372, National Institute of Economic and Social Research.

from the exercise of professional skills, so they tend to be less dependent on the organisation than other staff. Retaining their commitment can be difficult. They need to be given satisfying work to do, a good manager, and pay that they can see is fair in terms of their performance, or they will go elsewhere[118].

So how does an employer deliver on the psychological contract? First, it needs a relationship of trust with its employees, so that it can set up the right expectations. But what after that?

What managers do seems to have different effects on different employees, and therefore a broad range of interventions is needed if everyone is to be reached. These might include:

- Good recruitment and selection (not simply to get the right people in place, but to surround them with competent, encouraging colleagues as well)
- Training and development (the opportunity, the resources, and the push to take them up)
- Career opportunities (like promotion – and therefore filling posts from within, where feasible)
- Information-sharing and two-way communication
- Involvement in decisions
- Teamworking
- Tackling poor performance (it is not just bad for the bottom line in itself, but also puts unfair burdens on colleagues)
- An individual appraisal system (with not just an annual meeting, but proper goals and frequent review sessions)[119]
- Satisfactory pay and pensions

---

[118] Purcell J, Kinnie N, Hutchinson S, Rayton B and Swart J, 2003, *Understanding the People and Performance Link: unlocking the black box*, CIPD London, pp 68-69.
[119] A lot but not enough is known about appraisal systems: see eg Landy F J and Farr J L, 1980, "Performance Rating", *Psychological Bulletin*, vol. 87 no. 1, pp. 72-107.

- Job security
- Jobs that offer challenge and autonomy
- Good work-life balance[120].

It also seems to help if there is a keen awareness of what the organisation stands for, driven through all its levels and teams, which is capable of giving people-management policies focus and purpose; whether this is expressed in a formal mission statement is irrelevant[121].

How realistic is all this? Evidence in Britain is that people's expectations are not being met all that well. A large-scale study in a local authority in 1996 found that as many as the majority of employees were experiencing breach of the psychological contract[122]. A cross-sectoral study in 2002 found that about a third of people thought that their employer had not properly delivered on promises to ensure fair treatment by managers, to consult on changes affecting them, and to offer interesting work, while a quarter thought the same about promises to give fair pay and career opportunities. Over half the sample in this study said they trusted their immediate boss to look after their interests, which is fairly encouraging; but this figure fell to a third for senior management, which is less so. Still, most people felt

---

[120] This is a list of characteristics identified in research by a Bath University team, and should not be seen as exclusive. All of them should be judged comparatively rather than absolutely: so, for example, in a boom people may expect complete job security for staff who are competent, while in a depression they may simply look for better job security than in the next organisation, or at least for redundancies to be managed with great fairness.

[121] Purcell &c, 2003, pp 8, 13 *et seqq*. Not so easy – at a workshop, the Brazilian entrepreneur Ricardo Semler once asked 56 CEOs of Fortune 500 companies to write down their company beliefs statement, and most of them then agreed that they could not distinguish between the results (Semler R, 2003, *The Seven Day Weekend*, Random House, London, p 112).

[122] This may be a relatively high figure, since the work was done at the time of a public expenditure squeeze during which managers may have been obliged against their will to abandon previous commitments.

loyalty to their organisation, and were proud to tell others where they worked[123].

It is notable that, while this staff survey is generally consistent with a survey of employers the previous year, the latter revealed that employers had a much rosier view than their staff of the career opportunities in their organisations. Thus employers did not necessarily have an accurate perception of employees' attitudes and expectations[124]. Moreover, both these surveys were done over a decade ago, and after several years of an economic depression one might think that things would now be even less satisfactory than they were then.

The big message from the work described here is that people-management really is at the heart of whether employees perform well or not. It is not something to be left to the HR department (though HR managers ought to have the skills to support it through planning and training): it should be at the forefront of every manager's mind, and needs the time and attention of managers at all levels.

Management of people and performance

An incidental finding in the 1996 study was that supervisors themselves were frustrated at being unable to deliver on promises they had made to staff (eg on training)[125]: this highlights the importance in management training and communication of seeing that there is congruence between expectations centrally and locally within an organisation, notably on resource issues. More simply, the moral is that it is important not to over-promise.

---

[123] *Pressure at Work and the Psychological Contract*, 2002, Guest D E and Conway N, CIPD, London, p 21.

[124] *Employer Perceptions of the Psychological Contract*, 2001, Guest D E and Conway N, CIPD, London, p ix.

[125] Coyle-Shapiro J and Kessler I, 2000, "Consequences of the Psychological Contract for the Employment Relationship: a large scale survey", *Journal of Management Studies* 37 p 922;

Many people are dissatisfied with their work because of stress. Stress is a relatively new issue in management studies, having become prominent in the literature only in the 1970s. At first it seemed to be about things like time pressures, role ambiguity, uncertainty about boundaries, overpromotion or underpromotion, lack of job security, poor relations with the boss, lack of control over work, and office politics[126].

Then it expanded. Psychologists struggle with stress: it tends to be used as a portmanteau into which an unhelpfully large range of problems gets stuffed, from bullying to obesity to boredom to noise. A quarter of workers say their jobs are "very stressful", and stress is higher for more senior people and those working long hours, as well as those in the health and local government sectors[127]. And it does not help that people's work can be affected by stress not just at work, but also in their private lives, where the writ of managers does not run. As a result, people can think that there is little real possibility of dealing with it effectively.

Moreover, results of research are confusing. Things which are often associated with stress do not seem always to be so (such as one's own control over one's work[128]). And when stress is seen at a similar time to something else it is by no means always clear which causes which, or whether both are caused by some third factor (do people who are stressed at work feel discouraged from taking exercise, or do

Stress

---

[126] Cooper C L and Marshall J, 1976, "Occupational sources of stress: a review of the literature relating to coronary heart disease and mental ill-health", *Journal of Occupational Psychology*, vol 49 pp 11-28.

[127] *Pressure at Work and the Psychological Contract*, 2002, Guest D E and Conway N, CIPD, London.

[128] e.g. Smith A *et al.*, 2000, *The Scale of Occupational Stress: The Bristol Stress and Health at Work Study*, Health and Safety Executive; Vaananen A, Koskinen A, Joensuu M, *et al.*, 2008, "Lack of predictability at work and risk of acute myocardial infarction: an 18-year prospective study of industrial employees", *American Journal of Public Health*, vol 98, pp 2264-2271.

people who don't take exercise feel less able to cope with work?).

This does not mean that such confusions cannot be worked through. Careful thought about the nature of team-working, for example, has brought better understanding. It had long been accepted that empowering teams to improve their own work processes often leads both to greater employee satisfaction and to improved output efficiency. However, the recent extension of work process standardisation, in the form of just-in-time techniques or contact centre scripting, suggested that even in the contexts which lay claim to teamwork approaches, such as in Nissan or Mazda, there are indications of reduced rather than increased worker autonomy, and that such labour intensification causes stress and discontent[129].

Consideration has teased out key differences between the two cases – the first involving teams empowered to implement change as well as plan it, the latter only to propose changes on which management will dispose; and the first tending to be composed of different specialists (such as sport or medical teams), the second of interchangeable members[130]. Even though these relationships have not yet been empirically verified, this is very helpful. But there is a long way to go before such analysis could come up with practical advice across the whole problem identified as "stress".

Nevertheless, in the 1990s the Health and Safety Executive courageously tackled it. They sponsored research[128] and came up with a series of management standards which

---

[129] Slaughter J, 1987, "The team concept in the US auto industry: implications for unions", *Labour Notes*; Sewell G and Wilkinson B, 1992, "Empowerment or emasculation? Shopfloor surveillance in a total quality organisation", in Blyton P and Turnbull P (*edd.*) *Reassessing Human Resource Management*, London, Sage, pp 97-115.

[130] Legge K, 2005, *Human Resource Management: Rhetorics and Realities*, Palgrave Macmillan, Basingstoke, pp 260-266.

practitioners have accepted as sensible (although it is true that, some years later, these seemed to have had less effect in practice than they might have hoped[131]).

Thus the picture in relation to stress is blurred. There is sound evidence that many of the things which tend to get grouped under the label of "stress" are damaging and to be avoided, and that there is also interaction between the demands made on people at home and at work[132].

It is pretty obvious that there is not one solution to these problems. On the other hand, teasing them apart and finding appropriate remedies is not at all easy. Two kinds of intervention seem to be particularly helpful. One is reducing uncertainty and confusion, and the other relieving the impact of overall pressures at work.

Uncertainty tends to arise from the nature of the job and from day-to-day events in it. Some jobs are intrinsically more unpredictable than others (and knowledge of this can be put to good use in recruitment selection). But often the uncertainty in a job can be reduced by managing well. If managers are consistent towards their staff, and explain any inconsistencies openly and carefully; if distractions from the task are reduced through control of the working environment and resolution of unnecessary conflict between staff; and if jobs are carefully designed and their requirements and objectives communicated – then such steps will go a long way to reduce confusion, and help people to focus on doing what needs to be done well[133].

Overall pressures at work are generally best addressed through ensuring enough opportunities for recreation. Some

---

[131] Webster S & Buckley P, 2008, *Psychosocial Working Conditions in Britain in 2008*, Health and Safety Executive; Chandola T, 2010, *Stress at Work*, British Academy.

[132] This applies to men as well as women: see Woods D, *The extent of working fathers' stress levels revealed by new research*, HR Magazine, 5 November 2010, reporting research by Caroline Gatrell of Lancaster University Management School.

[133] Grant A M, Fried Y, Parker S K and Frese M (*edd*), 2010, *Journal of Organizational Behavior*, special issue "Putting Job Design in Context".

jobs, such as air traffic control, involve such intense and continuous concentration that frequent breaks are required[134]; but this is unusual. More widely, it is worth bearing in mind that breaks and time off are much more effective if taken frequently than if saved up and taken in large blocks. Thus the restorative effect of a holiday lasts on average no more than four weeks, while daily opportunities for recreation are very important – and physical exercise such as swimming or cycling is much more effective than time spent in unengaging activities such as watching television[135].

There have been several (albeit pretty extreme) cases of organisations having to pay up to £175,000 for not taking action to prevent excessive pressure of work, bullying, or lack of proper training. You will be well advised to look at the HSE management standards and think about what you might do to move closer towards them: things like making clear what's expected of people (and sticking to it), informing them and listening to them, and having clear policies against bullying, will at worst keep you out of the employment tribunal, and at best will make your team not only more productive, but a happier place for you and them to work in.

It is argued that contracting out support functions transfers staff to an organisation where their role is core

---

[134] In the case of air traffic control, typically of 30 minutes after each 1½ or 2 hours.

[135] Sonnentag S, 2011, *Staying Well and Proactive: The Importance of Everyday Recovery Processes*, paper delivered to Organisational Behaviour Seminar, Judge Institute for Management Studies, University of Cambridge, 12 December 2011. The present author has found that, if someone stays in the office after ordinary working hours, German managers tend to think that they cannot do their job during the time set and have a performance problem, while British managers tend to be impressed by their dedication. This anecdotal suggestion of the ill-success of presenteeism is borne out by a number of studies which suggest that performance falls away during the working day – and also by the fact that German labour productivity, of course, is higher than British.

business, and so improves motivation. But it can have other effects that operate in the other direction, such as

Contract-ing out regimentation of work[136]. And clients do not necessarily benefit, as was discovered by the organisation which gave its computer maintenance to a firm which found it more cost-effective to stop sending technicians to fix computers, and instead to collect faulty workstations for repair, leaving their hapless users computerless for days[137]. Across sectors it is now being viewed with more disfavour, and *The Economist* remarked recently "It has now become clear that outside firms usually cannot do boring back-office work any better and often do it worse. Many offshore outsourcing relationships have proved disappointing and some have ended in lawsuits"[138].

Targets A real discovery in the field of motivation was the impact of targets[139]. Interest in targets began in the 1950s, when Peter Drucker published ground-breaking work on "management by objectives", and set out eight areas in business where key targets ought to be set: market position,

---

[136] My own impression – no more than that – is that the Home Office has put its foot in it a lot more often since it became a Ministry of Law Enforcement, instead of the former rather charming Ministry of Everything Else where career officials could temper their experience of prisons and police with time spent working on animal welfare, broadcasting, taxi licensing or relations with the Isle of Man.

[137] Overell S, 2011, "Who's Pulling the Strings?", *The Guardian, Work* section, 27 August 2011 pp 1-2.

[138] *Economist*, Special Report on Outsourcing & Offshoring, 19 January 2013, p 12.

[139] Guzzo R A, Jette R D and Katzell R A, 1985, "The effects of psychologically based intervention programs on worker productivity: a meta-analysis", *Personnel Psychology*, 38, 275-91; Carson P P, Carson K D, Heady R B, 1994, "Cecil Alec Mace: The man who discovered goal-setting", *International Journal of Public Administration*, Volume 17, Issue 9 1994, pages 1679-1708; Locke E A, Saari L M, Shaw K N, Latham G P, 1981, "Goal Setting and Task Performance: 1969-1980", *Psychological Bulletin*, vol 90 no 1 pp 125-152; Latham G P and Locke E A, 1991, "Self-Regulation through Goal Setting", *Organizational Behavior and Human Decision Processes*, vol 50, pp 212-247. There is an excellent essay on the contemporary debate on targets at Meekings A, Briault S and Neely A, 2010, "Are your Goals Hitting the Right Target?", *LBS Business Strategy Review*, vol 21 issue 3 pp 46-51.

innovation, efficiency, resources, profit, management, worker performance and public responsibility[140].

This led to outstanding empirical research on motivation in the 1960s and 1970s, which firmly established that people seek purpose and things to do, and that when they are set goals they work harder trying to reach them. It has been found that where the goals set are of good quality, this makes people less distracted about reaching them, and also encourages them to put in more effort to get there, to persist longer in the task, and to exercise more ingenuity in doing it (such as planning better, or seeking out help). There is also a lot known about what makes a good target[141].

However, goals can also go badly wrong. Damage was notoriously done in the 1990s by over-enthusiasm with introducing what has been called the New Public Management approach[142]. Less in favour now (at least in its original form)[143], this sought to extend perceived private sector efficiencies to the public sector, through improved measurement of outputs and goal-setting, disaggregating organisations, replacing hierarchies with contractual relations, and the introduction of competitive mechanisms.

Many of the results were positive, but the move struggled with a series of unexpected consequences. One of the most important resulted from the fact that (although no organisation has only a single objective, since it has at least to balance a long-term goal with a short-term one) political objectives are often much more multifaceted than com-

---

[140] Drucker P F, 1954, *The Practice of Management*, Harper & Row.

[141] Guzzo R A and Gannett B A, 1988, "The Nature of Facilitators and Inhibitors of Effective Task Performance", in Schoorman F D and Schneider B (*edd.*), *Facilitating Work Effectiveness*, Lexington, pp 21-41.

[142] James O and Manning N, 1996, "Public Management Reform: a global perspective", *Politics* vol. 16(3) pp 143-149; Clark J, Gewirtz S and McLaughlin E (*edd.*), 2000, *New Managerialism, New Welfare?*

[143] Dunleavy P, Margetts H, Bastow S and Tinkler J, 2005, "New Public Management is dead: long live digital-era governance", *Journal of Public Administration Research and Theory* 16 pp 467-494.

mercial ones. This made it much more common for simple goal-setting to produce unwanted results in the public sector (eg hospital lunches were delivered more promptly, but patients did not have time to eat them and their health declined); while, when more targets were added to deal with these side-effects, the total number of goals mushroomed to the point where monitoring and reporting on them started to distract people from the business task, and managers would give up in despair.

We have all suffered from the call centre staff who cut you off abruptly in order to meet their call-time target. We know the horror stories of hospitals getting round targets for waiting time in A&E by leaving patients queuing on trolleys or in ambulances. We may have met councillors or head-teachers baffled by the way that the Government expected them to meet hundreds of apparently inconsistent targets in one particular service.

Good goals are drawn up with a focus on the big picture, yet framed precisely so as to tell one clearly whether they have been reached or not; they have a clear timescale; they are not too many to cope with; and they are difficult and stretching, but still within people's capacity. They're also reviewed at sensible intervals to make sure they're still right. Good goal setting (and holding people to account for reaching them or not) is probably the most important part of performance management, and maybe of engagement overall.

Pay What about reward? After the banks were rescued by the taxpayer, we became depressingly familiar with the argument that bankers need lots and lots of money to motivate them to work hard. Is that true? And have you noticed how rarely the same argument seems to extend to the people who work in the banks' call centres?

Of course, people have recognised since time immemorial that if you promise people rewards for working better or faster it will often produce results; and behaviourist science has stood by and applauded. But the more we go beyond that generalisation the more problematic it seems, leading to conclusions such as "Not only do financial incentives operate with different efficacy in different situations, but often they do not even lead to increased production"[144]. A major study has found that pay can do more than anything else to improve performance, but that the effect can also be negative[145].

Work fifty years ago found that personnel departments when administering pay were relying "on faddish and assumptive practices which lack empirical support"[146]. Although the word "assumptive" is a bit puzzling (can it be something to do with the Virgin Mary?), one nevertheless gets the drift; and it's not all that clear that things are now much better than they were then.

For example, a recent study by a Harvard team, of a UK system giving GPs financial rewards for performance in managing hypertension, found that it simply had no effect[147]. This fits with the generalisation we met earlier in this chapter, that paying too little will often create problems, while paying bonuses rarely does a lot of good. One recent writer revives an old remark to say that bonuses are actually

---

[144] Opsahl R L and Dunnette M D, 1966, "The role of financial compensation in industrial motivation", *Psychological Bulletin*, vol. 66, pp 94-118; a major recent study with similar results is Jenkins G D Jr., Mitra A, Gupta N, & Shaw J D, 1998, "Are Financial Incentives Related to Performance? A meta-analytic Review of Empirical Research.", *Journal of Applied Psychology*, 83, pp. 777-787.

[145] Guzzo R A, Jette R D and Katzell R A, 1985, "The effects of psychologically based intervention programs on worker productivity: a meta-analysis", *Personnel Psychology*, vol 38 pp 275-91.

[146] Dunnette M D and Bass B M, 1963, "Behavioral scientists and pesonnel management", *Industrial Relations*, vol 2 pp 115-130.

[147] Serumaga B *et al.*, 2011, "Effect of pay for performance on the management and outcomes of hypertension in the United Kingdom: interrupted time series study", *British Medical Journal*, 25 January 2011.

demotivating, inasmuch as people will do what they need to get the reward but then no more[148]. A recent large survey showed increasing worries among HR professionals and consultants that reward was not engaging employees[149]. And it is a commonplace observation that people will put huge amounts of effort and enthusiasm into their hobbies, for which they get paid nothing at all.

Frederick Taylor, the founder of "scientific management", believed that piece-work payment produced the best motivation. Piece-work is still a preferred method of payment for some repetitive unskilled or semi-skilled tasks, such as harvesting fruit and vegetables, sewing garments or following call-centre scripts.

But it needs to be treated very carefully: its motivational effects are often more complicated than they seem at first sight, whether because of innate limitations or because of employees responding by trying to game the system. For example, if rates are set too low workers may work slowly in the hope that they will be raised to improve the incentive; a mix of hourly pay and piece-rate bonus may discourage output by reducing the reward per item produced; if for any reason the employer feels obliged to lower the piece rate, this is seriously demotivating. And most basically, if there are any quality elements in the task, then quality may go down in response to piece-rate payment (and in some contexts, such as call centres, this can have far-reaching effects, such as mis-selling which ends up costing huge sums in compensation)[150].

Similar problems can emerge in circumstances where commission is paid, as is often the case with sales. Such cases can involve much more complex and responsible acti-

---

[148] Kohn A, 2003, *Punished by Rewards: The Trouble with Gold Stars, Incentive Plans, A's, Praise, and Other Bribes*, Houghton Mifflin.
[149] *CIPD Annual Survey Report, October 2012: Reward Risks*, p 5.
[150] Billikopf G E, 1985, "Response to Incentive Pay among Vineyard Workers", California Agriculture, vol 39-7, July-August, pp 13-14.

vities than most unskilled or semi-skilled tasks, and as a result the perverse incentives caused by most bonus or commission schemes can have very damaging (and costly) effects. On a wider stage, significant aspects of the 2006 financial meltdown can be attributed to this, and in the UK it has caused many people to be harmed by supposedly independent financial advice from agents paid by commission, which led such payments to be banned in the industry from 2013; explicit fixed fees have now to be negotiated.

In any event, in more and more jobs in a modern economy, the way that goods and services are made available is so complicated that any one person's "contribution" can seldom be objectively quantified. Often it has to be done by "merit pay" relying on subjective assessments by managers. But that raises other problems. First there are obvious risks of favouritism and corruption. But further, bonuses have little impact if they are kept small to reflect the fact that such assessments are inherently unreliable, while if they are made large to make sure they motivate then they arouse feelings of injustice, inspiring colleagues to resignation, or secret acts of revenge against the employer[151]. Further confusion is caused by the fact that, for cultural reasons, pay seems, in any event, to be a better motivator in the United States than elsewhere, which means, as usual, that research (most of which is done in the USA) can be misleading[152].

---

[151] Pearce J L, 1991, "Why Merit Pay Doesn't Work", in Steers R and Porter L (edd.), *Motivation and Work Behaviour*, McGraw-Hill; Kepes S et al., 2009, "Contingencies in the Effect of Pay Range on Organizational Effectiveness", *Personnel Psychology*, vol 62 pp 497-531; French S, Kubo K and Marsden D, 2002, "Why does performance pay de-motivate: financial incentives versus performance appraisal", in Hanami T, (ed.) *Universal wisdom through globalisation: selected papers from the 12th IIRA world congress*, Tokyo: Japan Institute of Labour Report 9: Japan Institute of Labour, Tokyo, Japan.

[152] Tosi H L and Greckhamer T, 2004, "Culture and CEO Compensation", *Organization Science*, vol 15 no 6 pp 657-670.

One of the most fundamental problems, however, is the increasing complexity of organisations, technical processes and markets, which means that with some exceptions workers are becoming increasingly unable to do their jobs without collaboration: incentivising their own task, at the expense of the help they give to others, can often actually be self-defeating. To quote a distinguished expert in this field:

> "Most kinds of organisation succeed because of co-operation among their members, not because of members' discrete, individual performances. Such co-operation is particularly critical among employees with valuable expertise or the discretion to commit the organisation's resources. It is simply not in the organisation's interest to encourage short-term single-transaction expectations among such important employees."[153]

So when one is faced with the question of what to do about reward, the truth seems to be, as in so many other fields of people management, that it depends on the circumstances. In a very simple job, people's output will respond directly to bonuses (as with piece work), provided the system is managed reasonably and does not lead to undue stress[154]. The more complex the job – and especially the more it involves teamwork, or action now for the sake of results in the longer term – pay must not become so low as to seem unfair, but if it rises above that level it is not likely to lead to much better results[155].

Whether bankers have a simple job or not…is a question I leave, dear reader, to you. For the moment, one thing which is indispensable in cultivating engagement is good communication, and that is what we now turn to.

---

[153] Pearce J L, 1991, "Why Merit Pay Doesn't Work", in Steers R and Porter L, *Motivation and Work Behavior*, McGraw-Hill, p. 505.

[154] Ganster D C, Kiersch C E, Marsh R E, Bowen A, 2011, "Performance-Based Rewards and Work Stress", *Journal of Organizational Behavior Management*, vol 31 no. 4 pp 221-235.

[155] In a term devised by Frederick Herzberg (1959, *The Motivation to Work*, New York: John Wiley and Sons) it becomes a "hygiene factor".

Chapter 5: Communication

This chapter looks at why and how communication becomes a problem in larger organisations, showing that successful communication needs to use a range of channels and to flow in both directions. It identifies the key roles of line managers and supervisors, and touches on why cost savings sometimes lead to difficulties, touching on the implications of open-plan offices.

An organisation with different divisions operating on the same site has just discovered as I write that one division has been making employees redundant while another has been recruiting similar labour from the market. This expensive and image-damaging process carried on despite the presence of a central personnel department!

Organization, John Child, 1976, p. 96

Scene: Paris. Manager, with big glasses on his nose, in front of graph heading sharply downwards (speaks in English): "Big Problem!"
Observer translates into French for the benefit of his colleague: "Il dit qu'il fait confiance à l'équipe pour trouver de nouvelles opportunités dans un context morose..." ("He says he can rely on the team to find new opportunities in a discouraging situation...")

Cartoon by Colcanopa, Le Monde newspaper (Paris), 3 July 2012, p. 10

Key message of this chapter: Communication is vital and underrated. It is also much studied, but more work is needed to get to really concrete results.

A huge amount of what is done in organisations involves communication. And this is not always for the obvious purposes of resolving disagreements, giving instructions and reporting on progress with tasks.

As organisations grow in size, they become more complex, and people in them become more specialised.

When an organisation becomes larger and more differentiated, communication links become more tenuous. The natural tendency is to communicate with others within the same department, with whom one shares common problems and experiences.

These common problems and experiences reinforce people's identity with their own specialised department at the expense of integrating with other departments in pursuit of an

overriding objective.
Organization, John Child, 1976, pp. 96-7

People at work focus on what is expected of them, and that is usually their own immediate outputs. Their day-to-day contacts are with their immediate colleagues, who have similar outputs expected of them. They develop a culture of looking within their teams rather than outside. This means that it is very easy for people to lose sight of the ultimate goals of the organisation, and even more of the possible contribution that people in *other* teams can make to these.

Hence the kind of problem we have all faced as a consumer, where, for example, we call up a company to place an order, and are kept for so long, running round an automated telephone system pressing buttons 1, 2 and 3, that in the end we curse, give up, and call another company instead. One imagines the IT department and the contact centre management congratulating themselves on the savings in staff costs, while all the time the sales and finance departments are puzzling over why the business results are so poor.

Sometimes structures can be set up to help overcome such problems, such as liaison committees or even dedicated liaison teams. But solutions of this sort can be costly. Worse, they tend not to work very well, as operational teams generally find it hard to see how they are related to their own priority objectives: they fail to take the point, and resent the time they spend on them.

Hence management have a key part to play in addressing this issue. They need to do so in two ways. One is by acting as channels of communication themselves[156]. The

---

[156]As was pointed out by the army engineer Henri Fayol, one of the pioneers of management theory, this follows a classic military command-and-control model under which it is only where lines of authority in a hierarchy converge that action can properly be taken to co-ordinate different tasks (Fayol H, 1916, *Administration industrielle et générale; prévoyance, organisation, commandement, coordination, controle*, Paris, H. Dunod et E. Pinat).

other is by encouraging and monitoring direct communication between the teams involved.

Put like that, it sounds obvious. But in practice it is not so easy. In a relentless search for cost savings, middle management layers have been stripped out of organisations wholesale since 1990. Hence there is no longer the capacity there once was for managers to channel and encourage communication. Those who do try, find that their work builds rapidly into long queues, creating unacceptable delays; they do not repeat the experiment. *Middle managers*

Direct communication between teams is often therefore the only practical solution. But this immediately runs into the problem that the design of any organisation fosters a culture which discourages such contact. It is hard for managers to see the strength of this culture, and they often fail to devote enough of their own time and attention to overcoming it. Senior managers need to be aware that this is not some floppy HR fad: it is a real issue which deserves space in their diary and that of the supervisors in their teams. Efforts can be made to get round the problem with structural adjustment, known as "matrix management"; but this also needs a lot of time put in if it is to work properly[157].

A related problem is often communication between managers and their staff. It is a particular difficulty among first-line supervisors – one of the most important roles so far as motivation and performance are concerned – since often people are promoted to this level because they have good technical skills, and then find themselves expected to manage other people without any aptitude, experience or training for this different task. Themselves, they have the experience and expertise to see easily what needs to be done, and they naturally expect their teams to do the same; they may even feel it may seem patronising to explain. Hence, often, they do not communicate much. *Supervisors*

---

[157] Davis S M and Lawrence P R, 1977, *Matrix*, Addison-Wesley, Massachusetts.

A further problem is that even in situations where task instructions are quite fully given (as is often the case in manufacturing, in clerical functions, in hospitals and in the armed forces), it is easy to fail to take the next step and provide a full understanding of the job and how it fits in to the organisation's remit. This is sometimes because of a misguided feeling that it may tempt people to invent less successful ways of doing things for which there is already an established routine. But giving such background inform-ation is important, and not only because it enables bridges for the inevitable gaps in instructions to be improvised in a sensible way. Often, more significantly, it is a great help with loyalty and engagement, since staff who feel trusted, and treated like adults, are more likely to make an effort for their employer[158].

Hence managers need to be aware that they *do* have to explain. In today's complex organisations they may have to explain a lot, including the historical background to a problem, the politics of relationships with clients or other delivery partners, and presentational or publicity pitfalls.

They also need to bear in mind that different people take things in differently. Some can manage a lot of information at once, while others need it repeated several times. Some remember things they are told face to face more easily than things written down on a piece of paper, others are the other way round[159]. You need to tailor your delivery to your audience, many times; and the more complex the message, the more often you will need to repeat it on different occasions and using different media. Checking that people understand what is wanted is also essential (always with

---

[158] Katz D and Kahn R L, *The Social Psychology of Organizations*, 1966, Wiley, London, pp. 239-243; see previous chapter.
[159] There is not however an effective formal way of identifying people's capacities in this area: see above on Learning Styles, in the chapter on Skills.

tact, since people who think they might look foolish won't necessarily admit to not having taken a message in).

Another important aspect of communication to staff is feedback on performance. This also has its difficulties. Often the manager prefers to see his role as leading rather than punitive, while the managed is happy to hear praise but not blame. Hence there is a tendency for meetings reviewing performance to be put off to a point at which they become *really* difficult[160]. It is vital that they are made routine and frequent, and among the highest priority items in the diary – yet if they get too routine they become perfunctory events with no impact. A focus on information exchange, goal review and skill improvement will take the edge off them if needed, but it is really important that if there are problems or misunderstandings they are addressed explicitly and promptly.

Performance monitoring and review

Getting information back is critical as well. It is insufficient to give someone a task and then go away and come back expecting it to have been done. There needs to be reporting of progress so that managers know that things are on track, and systems in place to deliver this. Moreover, any manager needs to be able to listen to the emotions behind what is being said to them, not just its formal content, so that they can tune their own communications effectively and ensure that their staff are engaged with what they are doing (this is sometimes called active listening[161]).

One of the most important areas of communication is between each staff member and his or her line manager. It is firmly established that the line manager relationship is critically important to people at work. For most staff their

[160] Katz D & Kahn R L, *ibid.*

[161] Rogers C R, and Farson R E, 1991, *Active Listening*: reprinted in Kolb D A, Rubin I M, and Osland J S (*edd.*), 1991, *The Organisational Behavior Reader,* pp. 187-199.

line manager is the spokesman for what the organisation wants of them, what it thinks of them, and how it values them. How their line manager behaves is a major factor in their performance, in their commitment and morale, and in whether they stay or move on. Hence line managers must be effective at communicating with their staff. Unlike senior management, they generally share a workspace, or at least a building, with their staff, which means that frequent informal communication ought to be easy enough.

First-line managers were intensively studied in the immediate post-war years, largely in the USA at the University of Michigan, though various challenges showed the promising early results to have been less conclusive than had been hoped[162]. But times have changed. The foremen who were studied were at that time balanced in a sensitive position between managers and a unionised, often militant workforce, and they usually worked in a noisy factory where social or subtle communication was impossible. Today's supervisors tend to be responsible for a larger number of people, and subject to more complex and demanding measurements of their outputs, yet are still expected to motivate their teams in addition to their functional roles.

Thus organisational structures can be vital in ensuring the right communication, since staff effort, courtesies and loyalties have a tendency to stop at organisational bound-aries, and matrix management systems designed to

Struct-ures

overcome this seldom work well for long[163].

Myself, as a civil servant I moved for a while from Whitehall to the Scottish Office, and was much impressed by the integration of government policy in Scotland, which was much better than in London. Part of this was down to

---

[162] Rose M, 1975, *Industrial Behaviour: theoretical development since Taylor*, Penguin Books, Harmondsworth, pp 153, 164-167.
[163] Davis S M and Lawrence P R, 1977, *Matrix*, Addison-Wesley, Massachusetts.

the Scottish Office being quite small and intimate, and many of the senior staff having been to the same handful of schools and universities; but it was largely, I think, due to the senior organisational structures, which were such that departmental barriers were always breached at some level, while in Whitehall they went right up to the top.

Thus the (civil servant) head of a Whitehall department would report to a (politician) Secretary of State with the same remit at a political level; while in Edinburgh the head of a department would report to two junior ministers, each of whom would have responsibility for matters within the remit of another official head of department as well (*Fig. 1*). This meant that, whether you were an official or a minister,

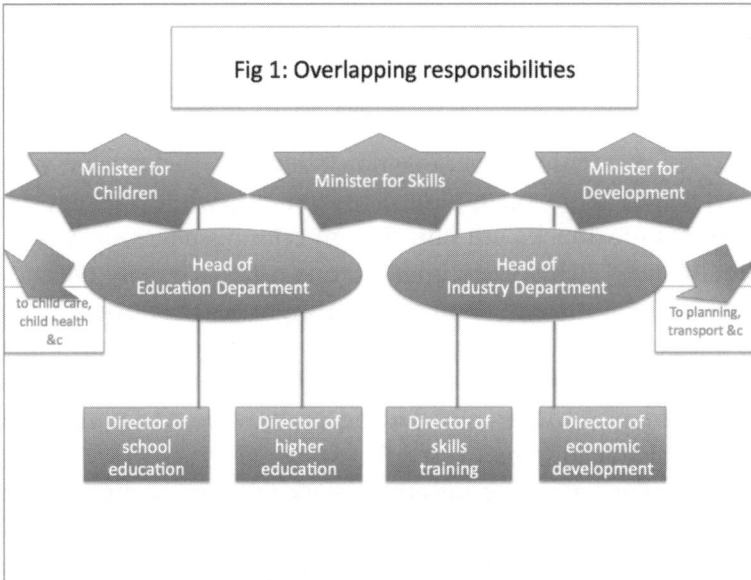

Fig 1: Overlapping responsibilities

there was always someone who saw beyond your own horizon, and was able to put the ambitions and anxieties of your own services into proportion. It is telling that, after devolution, when a more conventional structure was put in place to massage devolved ministers' egos by giving each their own dedicated ministry, an effectiveness review found that departmentalism was rampant. This is an example of how important organisational structure can be.

Open-plan offices

Office layout is important in enabling or hindering communication. Hence, in many organisations, the tendency of top management's offices to congregate together, like aristocrats' houses in earlier days clustering round the royal palace. Open plan working is one of the main recent innovations in this area. It makes informal communication a good deal easier, though it also makes it more public: subversive remarks are made less safely in open-plan than while passing in the corridor. The fierce resistance which greeted its introduction in the 1990s has now softened a bit, probably as people have better learned to use email, which covers some of the gaps which the change set up. But research does show that distraction is a much greater problem than people realise.

As a crude generalisation, routine tasks are best performed in an open-plan environment, while managerial and technical tasks are not, though circumstances do vary a good deal[164]. However, open-plan is usually hugely cheaper than cellular offices, so in an era of tight cost control there is a judgement to be made whether to put up with some blunting of performance for the sake of the very concrete cost savings. Much may depend on how near to perfection the results need to be.

Similar issues are raised by working from home: people whose relationships with their managers are largely virtual have been found to get less effective support from them than

---

[164] Oldham G R and Brass D J, 1979, "Employee Reactions to an Open-Plan Office: A Naturally Occurring Quasi-Experiment", *Administrative Science Quarterly*, vol 24 no 2 Jun; Hedge A, 1982, "The Open-Plan Office: A Systematic Investigation of Employee Reactions to Their Work Environment", *Environment and Behavior*, September 1982 vol 14 no 5, pp 519-542; Maher A and von Hippel C, 2005, "Individual differences in employee reactions to open-plan offices", *Journal of Environmental Psychology*, vol 25, issue 2 June, pp 219-229.

when they frequently meet face to face, and working from home also tends to be an impediment to training and development – quite apart from isolating people from the more interesting office gossip[165].

Extremely important though communication is, it should not be seen as the answer to all problems. There is a rationalist myth that conflict always results from poor communication, and that if communication were only improved it would go away[166]. But, as we all really know, conflict can also result from a range of other causes, ranging from prejudice and revenge, to clashes of interests or values. And attempting to reconcile such conflicts simply with the aid of better communications will not meet with success: there are times when harder decisions need to be made. So next we look at conflict.

---

[165] Golden T and Fromen A, 2011, "Does it matter where your manager works? Comparing managerial work mode (traditional, telework, virtual) across subordinate work experiences and outcomes", *Human Relations*, 64 (11), 1451-1475

[166] This myth is especially visible in some parts of the education and social services worlds, though it is by no means exclusive to the public sector: Adam Smith and Milton Friedman attached at least as much weight to rational choice in human decision-making as did Karl Marx. See Katz D and Kahn R L, 1966, *The Social Psychology of Organisations*, pp. 224 *et seqq*; cp. Newcombe T M, 1947, "Autistic hostility and social reality", *Human Relations*, vol 1, pp. 69-86.

Chapter 6: Conflict

This chapter looks at how conflict can be among the most positive as well as the most negative events in organisations. It touches on cultural issues, the role of diversity and the risks of unanimity, and the problem that stress poses in this context.

Many facts of organisational life can be readily understood if the model of organisations is one which views social patterns not as fixed and rigid interrelations but as the outcome of a continuing tug of war.
The Social Psychology of Organizations, D Katz and R L Kahn, 1965

Key message of this chapter: Conflict is both bad and good, but is not well understood. Few people know how to deal with it, and others need help – which is available.

Many people will run a mile from conflict. Some, who seem to thrive on it, can be looked on rather suspiciously by their colleagues.

Costs and benefits of conflict
For many years the prevailing view was that all conflict is bad. Where it was accepted as inevitable, such as the letting of contracts or changes to terms of employment, it was hedged about with complex procedures to defuse its explosive potential. Dealing with these has become a specialist industry, and we don't address such negotiations in this book: this chapter is about the rather murkier area of conflict between people and groups within organisations, its potential for good and bad, and how it is handled.

For conflict in organisations is a good thing, not a bad thing, provided it is well managed and well used. Work is important to people. They hold different beliefs about it. Sometimes they believe them passionately for the sake of truth and their organisation's future (and sometimes, too, because their own positions and careers depend on them). In some cases such differences lead to feelings of threat and hostility, and paralysing, entrenched positions where everyone is locked in the past, endlessly re-fighting old battles. But in others they are a source of new ideas, letting organisations take fresh directions and adapt effectively to a changing world. Hence, resolving differences does not just avoid derailment, but encourages creativity. Doing it well is essential, if organisations are to survive and flourish.

For there are, as we all know, different ways of approaching conflict. Psychologists now tend to see these as falling into four or five different patterns, namely: avoidance; confrontation; compliance; and compromise, or perhaps better a problem-solving approach which seeks to maximise advantages to everyone. Each of these approaches can be useful in certain circumstances[167]. And any particular conflict can be handled well or badly.

Feelings of hostility need to be controlled and defused. However, constructive disagreements need to be both encouraged and channelled, so that they stimulate creativity and effectiveness without undermining loyalty and commitment. Developing the right social norms and expectations is central in enabling this, and handling this process is one of the most important of leadership tasks at all levels of an organisation. For when it goes wrong the damage can be spectacular, as anyone who has spent any time in organisations knows very clearly.

How can we generalise like that? Studies in this area are difficult, because conflict is so integral to human experience that it is hard to isolate its effects from other measures[168], and though there was a brief period of interest in organisational conflict by scientists in the late 1960s it is only in the last twenty years that much work on it has been done. One especially large-scale study, however, has found some interesting results. In 2008 the British psychology consultancy OPP carried out a large world-wide survey on

---

[167] For example, compromise is often a good temporary solution, but a poor approach to resolving complex problems properly. The styles and their merits are helpfully set out by the current major work on organisational conflict: Rahim M A, 1992, *Managing Conflict in Organizations*, Westport CT, Praeger, pp 25 and 82.
[168] Rahim, 1992, *op. cit.* p 79.

workplace conflict[169]. Unsurprisingly, they found that conflict was universal. 85% of employees had to deal with conflict, and 29% did so "always" or "frequently".

But while 31% of managers thought they themselves handled conflict well, only 22% of their staff agreed. And nearly twice as many staff as managers thought that conflict could be and ought to be dealt with better than it was. This may be because managers think of conflict only when it affects them, and don't make themselves aware of other kinds of conflict – for the survey also found that managers thought that the main area of conflict was between line managers and their staff, while staff, to the contrary, felt that it was the customers who were the problem, with front-line roles being the most exposed to conflict.

Mismanaged conflict carries heavy costs. Any organisation would be glad of a 5% performance improvement. But about 5% of the time of staff in the UK was reported as spent on dealing with conflict. This was twice as much as in the Netherlands, but a good deal less than in the USA, and half as much as in Ireland or Germany. Moreover, conflicts often escalated (89% of staff had experienced this). Results of conflict ranged from personal insults or attacks (seen by 27% of employees), and sickness or absence (25%), to people leaving the organisation (18%) and project failure (9%).

Women were often more affected than men by the emotional consequences of conflict, including feeling they had to avoid certain colleagues, and the consequential hampering of team working. The charitable sector was the most affected by escalating conflicts, and twice as likely as

---

[169] *Fight, flight or face it?: celebrating the effective management of conflict at work* (2008) OPP with CPP and CIPD; preface by Robert McHenry. 5,000 full-time employees were surveyed across six western European countries, the USA and Brazil. The study does not define conflict, but it's not clear to me either that it helps much to classify it elaborately into ten different kinds (as is done for example on pages 22-23 of Rahim 1992 *op.cit.*).

the average to be affected by sickness or absence as a result (this may be influenced by volunteers, who will find it easier to avoid the pain by staying away from work, or to resist pressures to conform[170]). For half the HR staff surveyed, at least 10% of their time was spent dealing with conflict.

But what do these figures mean? If Germans spend four times as long dealing with conflict as Dutch people, does it mean that the wise Dutch are naturally collaborative and the foolish Germans pugnacious? Or does it mean that the sensible Germans put time into resolving resentments which the silly Dutch are always trying to sweep under the carpet, but which still sit there quietly festering and getting in people's way?

Of course, individuals do differ in how they approach conflicts, and may adopt different tactics in different cases. However, these very different perceptions in a large study show that generalisation about responses can be possible and helpful.

The main causes of conflict were seen as personality clashes (49%), stress (34%), heavy workloads (33%) and poor top leadership (29%). But this varied quite a lot between different countries. Brazilians saw clashes of values as much more significant than other nationalities, while in Germany it was accountability issues which seemed more prominent, and in France lack of honesty or openness. This points up the dangers of generalising, and the need for cultural sensitivity in managing conflict issues, especially in international firms or where immigrant workers are involved.

What helps with conflict management? Encouragingly, the OPP study found that training is helpful. It reported that in France and Belgium there was a low level of training at

---

[170] See Handy C, 1988, *Understanding Voluntary Organisations*, Penguin, Harmondsworth.

27% or 28% (and even then only half of it was seen as effective); this may have been a response to a relatively low level of conflict in those countries, but it does seem to have led to more negative outcomes where conflict did occur. In Brazil, on the other hand, where over twice as many staff received training (68%), there was a general expectation of positive results from conflict situations.

Training to deal with conflict

So far, all this might be just cultural – perhaps in the survey the words used in French to translate the English "conflict" carried overtones more threatening than those in Portuguese. But the team also found that the relationship in Brazil between training and positive expectations was so strong that there was a distinct statistical correlation between the two, which does suggest that training is worthwhile.

Another less certain factor was age. Overall, twice as many respondents thought older people handled conflict effectively as younger people. But there was also a tendency for everyone to say that people of their own age were the best at this, so it may be that there were simply more older people in the sample surveyed, and the results need to be treated cautiously.

Age

Of course, the easiest way of dealing with conflict is to make sure it doesn't happen at all. And in a lot of organisations the management find it helpful if the only people who join the board are those who are like the present members. This often used to be known as the "old school tie". That isn't quite so obvious these days, but it's common enough, all the same, for boards to be surprisingly homogeneous in sex, race or class background.

This is interesting, since it is an issue which people can be reluctant to unpack, since challenging such basic assumptions can be perceived as time-wasting, or worse. And it's quite true that people with similar backgrounds can get on well. In particular, they can communicate easily, since they "speak the same language": they have the same kinds of verbal codes and presuppositions which don't need to be articulated.

But that's exactly where the problem lies. Some in-groups are tolerant and creative, accepting of the differences of their members. But others are far from that, and develop a discipline and rigidity which blinkers them to new ideas or to changes in their environment that, in fact, may urgently need attention if the group is to survive and prosper. This has been called "groupthink"[171]. The term was coined in the context of the disastrous 1961 Bay of Pigs invasion of Cuba sponsored by the Kennedy administration in the US; but the phenomenon is, of course, an ancient and universal one.

Group-think

Studies of groupthink suggest that it tends to arise when people in a group enjoy a cosy and comfortable atmosphere, and therefore come to expect that they will easily reach complete agreement on every important issue. They come to feel invulnerable, they are complacent about their ethics, they ignore warnings or rationalise them away, and they stereotype outsiders. Thus they cultivate an illusion of unanimity, and they reinforce it with self-censorship, with pressure on dissidents, and by blocking inconsistent information. They don't tend to penalise critical thinking overtly: instead, they encourage members to internalise group norms so that it doesn't happen. In such circum-stances – as in Orwell's *Nineteen Eighty-Four*, of which the term "groupthink" was deliberately reminiscent – dissent becomes literally unthinkable. As a result, challenging ideas, new directions, and even the recognition that things are going wrong, all become impossible. This is very dangerous for any organisation.

However, analysis of groupthink has failed to provide a detailed description of how it operates. Critics of the idea

---

[171] Janis I L, 1971, "Groupthink", *Psychology Today*, November 1971, pp 43-46.

point out[172] that, though it meets the common sense test, it is hard to operationalise, it tends to explain at a high level of generalisation, and it addresses the psychology of the individuals involved, rather than the dynamics of the groups studied and the impact of their political and historical contexts.

Despite such criticisms, it is evident that, where there is insufficient challenge or variety of perspective, there are risks. Teams need to be led in a way which welcomes and values challenges, and which is supportive of the management time that is needed to address and resolve the resulting conflicts thoroughly. A systems perspective is often helpful in this (see page 93).

In general, too, teams need to have sufficient internal diversity to avoid these risks. This may involve the sort of groups that are the subject of recent equalities legislation, such as women or ethnic minorities; or it may involve less visible diversity characteristics such as a mix of arts and science graduates, or of extraverts and introverts. However, there is no doubt but that it's a good idea.

It is also vital for there to be institutions in place to protect victims where there is conflict: we all remember bad things at primary school, and ordinary people can be very cruel, especially if given power without status[173]. And, of course, a team whose attention is on bullying a scapegoat is not one which is focused on the job.

---

[172] Wekselberg V, 1996, "Groupthink: a triple fiasco in social psychology", in *Problems of theoretical psychology*, ed. Tolman C W, *et al.*, Captus Press, North York, Ontario, pp 217-226 [the word "fiasco" in the title here picks up the title of Janis's own 1972 book, *Victims of Groupthink: A psychological study of foreign-policy decisions and fiascoes*].
[173] Browning C R, 1992, *Ordinary Men – Reserve Police Battalion 101 and the Final Solution in Poland*, London, Harper Collins; Fast N J, Halevy N, Galinsky A D, 2011, *The destructive nature of power without status*, Journal of Experimental Social Psychology, Volume 48, Issue 1, January 2012, pages 391–394.

The backstop for such protection is employment law. But we all know that though that may be there for you if you can show that you were unfairly dismissed from your long-standing job, or not promoted simply because you were Jewish or black, there are nevertheless lots of cases where there is unfair prejudice but it is entirely personal, and the victim cannot claim the protection of the law.

Groups often define themselves in opposition to out-siders, as has been seen in Rwanda, Bosnia and countless other places in human history, but tragedies can be writ small in organisations as well as large in nations. People who belong to the wrong group, or who are simply different in some way, are often bullied at school by children who already ought to know better, and surprisingly many are bullied at work by adults who have had plenty of chances to learn better.

Malignant conflict

There is an overlap here with the psychology of the individual. Despite recent advances in neuroscience, we cannot see what is going on inside people's heads except in a physical sense, which limits our ability to demonstrate how mental processes work[174]. However, a number of models of these are well-known, and the explanations offered by the psychodynamic model are quite coherent.

Organisations contain people of many different kinds, and inevitably some of them have psychological problems. They may or may not have one of the twelve personality disorders classified by earnest American psychologists[175], but even if they don't they may show tendencies towards them. Any of these will interfere with ordinary social

---

[174] There has been major progress in neuroscience since the mid-1990s, and a great deal has been claimed for it as a result, but too much of this is at the wrong level to be very helpful – as if someone, asked to explain why a chess-playing computer moved its rook instead of its pawn, were to do it in terms of the electronics involved, rather than of the nature of a chess game.

[175] American Psychiatric Association, 2000, *Diagnostic and Statistical Manual of Mental Disorders*, 4th ed, Arlington, USA.

relations and hence has a potential to provoke conflict within working groups, and people suffering from some of them tend to be attracted to particular working roles (for example, a number of people in positions of authority, it has been argued, suffer from a degree of narcissism, which, like psychological splitting, can lead to destructive emotional behaviour and the depersonalisation of others[176]).

On the other hand, it would be silly to expect all employees to be Brave New World-type clones. Indeed, the diversity of our colleagues is what makes our teams work well, and creates the grit in the oyster which is also (as it were) a seed of change and creativity; too much agreement and trust within an organisation can lead to blindness to external change, and the kind of problems which Marks and Spencer fell into in the 1990s[177].

A problem resulting from recent tendencies towards the intensification of work is that they reduce the spare emotional capacity available to people to make allowances for difficult behaviour by others, and to maintain the social equilibrium of working groups. That makes it all the more important to address issues of conflict properly, rather than to avoid them and hope they will go away. This may be why we see in the OPP study strong evidence from Brazil and elsewhere that training in handling conflict is often a sound investment.

For turning a blind eye to conflict and hoping it will go away is not an option. Not least because all organisations are obliged all the time to deal with change, something which is occasionally exciting, but which in general we all resist vigorously...

---

[176] Diamond M A and Allcorn S, 2004, "Moral Violence in Organizations: Hierarchic Dominance and the Absence of Potential Space", *Organisational & Social Dynamics* 4(1), pp 22-45

[177] Hope-Hailey V, Searle R and Dietz G, 2012, *Where has all the trust gone?*, CIPD, Wimbledon, p 25.

Chapter 7: Change

This chapter warns how change often tends to be misused, and looks in some detail at how IT projects can illustrate the risks of change. It describes the principal models of successful change management, stressing the importance of communications, and explains how systems thinking is an especially helpful approach.

> *Caelum non animum mutant qui trans mare currunt.*
> *Travelling elsewhere may vary your surroundings, but it cannot change your character.*
>
> Q. Horatius Flaccus, *Epistles*

> *Change is inevitably to some extent an excursion into the unknown. It implies a commitment to future events that are not entirely predictable and to their consequences, and inevitably provokes doubt and anxiety. Any significant change within a social system implies changes in existing social relationships....It follows that any significant social change implies a change in the operation of the social system as a defence system. While this change is proceeding, anxiety is likely to be more open and intense. Resistance to social change can be better understood if it is seen as the resistance of groups of people unconsciously clinging to existing institutions because changes threaten existing social defences against deep and intense anxieties.*
>
> Isabel E. P. Menzies, *The Functioning of Social Systems as a Defence against Anxiety, 1961*

Key message of this chapter: There is good agreement on the basic principles of organisational change, but it requires good planning and resourcefulness.

Anthropologists warn us that there is always change of some sort in organisations: their environments and their people are constantly in flux, and they must respond to that fact – indeed, management would hardly be needed if this was not so. But there has been growing recognition in recent years that, when deliberate changes are made in how organisations are managed, this is often handled badly[178]. And this has rightly led to an increasing focus on change itself as a management issue.

---

[178] CIPD research suggests that less than 60% of re-organisations met their stated objectives, which were usually financial improvement (CIPD factsheet *Change management*, November 2010); see also Gardini *et al*, 2011, "Finding the right place to start change", *McKinsey Quarterly* [Nov], suggesting that in the private sector only one in three large-scale change programmes succeeds.

Change, like much of organisational life, has at least as much to do with emotion as with rational analysis: it is full of the risk of things going wrong, and therefore pretty scary. This is one reason why it is often handled badly: because people's fear of change makes them rush it, or not talk it through thoroughly enough before taking action.

There are three simple mistakes which can be made about change. If they have a common theme, it is under-estimating the complexity of the process.

Errors in pressing change

First, change can be misused, as a badge of honour. New leaders, especially CEOs, often feel they have to justify their appointment by rushing into change: this will show that their predecessor left things in a mess, so that it's just as well that they themselves took over. But unnecessary change, even if well handled, can be hugely costly, diverting resources which would be much better put to other uses. And it also opens up needless risks, for example by disrupting cultural or communications practices which are working well and have taken years to develop.

Second, where the culture *does* need to change, it can be assumed that the problem can be fixed by just issuing notices, or sending people on a "sheep-dip" training course. This is a misunderstanding of what that sort of training can achieve. It is a good way of making sure that everyone takes in new rules about health and safety, or how a move to new offices will work. But it will not by itself impart even complex skills, much less changes in attitudes and beliefs. It may, of course, give people the right vocabulary to use if they want to pretend that change has happened – but that will only disguise the original problem, rather than solve it[179].

---

[179] See eg Davies I K, 1971, *The Management of Learning*, London, McGraw-Hill; Rackham N and Morgan T, 1977, *Behavioural Analysis in Training*, Maidenhead, McGraw-Hill.

Third, structural change is often asked to carry a load it cannot bear. The new CEO who needs results quickly, and results which are visible to everyone, often decides that it's the organisational structure that needs changing. Superficially, this has a number of advantages. Organisational structures can be changed, if not quite at the stroke of a pen, *Temptation to* then pretty quickly – a lot faster than changing people's *struct-* skills or the organisational culture (the tiresome tailwork of *ural* putting the website right can be delegated to IT). Such *change* changes are also easily visible both inside and outside the organisation, and give vivid evidence of the dynamism of the leader responsible. As a bonus, they will also give an opportunity, in the distribution of new posts, to reward friends and punish enemies.

In the real world, however, structural changes do not necessarily make a great deal of real difference. Most things can continue to be done somehow regardless of the organisational structure. And if there is inefficiency, or a poor skillset, or endemic conflict, or a reluctance to face reality in some way, then changes to the organisational structure will not make the situation any better. On the contrary, they may well be an unhelpful distraction from the real problem.

Moreover, structural change is generally costly. It needs planning, consultation, communication and delivery. It often demands consultancy input, maybe a lot of it. And the amount of staff time it takes – in managing the change itself, in the downturn in output resulting from the stress it causes, in recruitment and redundancy, and in the forging of new relationships and in people's training and habituation into new roles – is enormous, and generally a good deal more than expected.

One thing is often overlooked and helps to make the results of change uncertain: that, whatever our position in an organisation, we only see a small part of it, and we use that to make assumptions about what the rest of it is like. Thus we do not see all the links that relate the parts of the organisation to each other, and also to the world outside (such as customers, competitors, regulators). Hence, when we see a problem which can be resolved by change, it is easy for us to take action which will improve the part of the organisation which we see, but difficult for us to avoid unexpected or even damaging change to the parts we don't.

This is obvious in relation to major IT improvements. Generally, when a new IT system is mooted, the IT specialists know what the IT can do, and line management know what work needs to be done. However, the IT specialists don't know enough about the work to suggest in detail how the IT could help, and line management don't know enough about the IT to suggest what it might be able to help with. Moreover, introducing an IT system generally doesn't mean just doing the things you did before, but using keyboards instead of quill pens: it usually means tackling a lot of tasks quite differently, so as to take advantage of the opportunities the IT offers – processes are often revolutionised, and the people who do them must be grouped differently with new managers, need fresh skills, or may even have to be replaced. Finally, IT specialists have developed a professional language, inventing new words like "functionality" and "middleware" and using old words like "application" and "client" in new ways, which line management can find it hard to follow. Conversely, external IT consultants (which you usually need) don't understand the local language of the line managers. Therefore it's quite obvious that a major dialogue will be needed before a new IT system can be properly planned.

IT project failures So it is astonishing how many IT initiatives are launched without such a process. And less than surprising that so many major IT initiatives cost more than was planned, take longer than people thought, or even just fail altogether. Project management has improved greatly to deal with such problems, notably with PRINCE2[180]; but that is still a dark art that often seems to have more to do with politics than with science. Moreover, as PRINCE2 recognises clearly, IT is only a special case: all projects need management, whether IT projects or not, and all project management and change management is tricky.

The National Programme for IT in the NHS is a recent and the biggest example of a project that ran into problems. It was launched in June 2002 to cost £12.4bn and to be completed by 2010, the main component being care records to be completed by 2007; the major supplier was Fujitsu. A National Audit Office report in June 2006 reported good progress, but also some concerns. By May 2008 it had become very clear that there was delay; indeed, the care records were now expected to slip to 2015. On 6 December 2009, in response to the global financial crisis, the Labour Government announced that the project was to be scaled back to save £600m; on 10 September 2010 the Coalition Government announced further scaling back to save another £700m.

In May 2011 the NAO reported that care records had still only been implemented in some areas, and that different systems were being delivered in different places. There had been a major conflict about additional work, which Fujitsu claimed resulted from new requirements, and the Government from Fujitsu's failure to deliver; as a result the contract had been transferred to BT, which of course caused further delay. Costs were held down, but at the expense of reductions of about a quarter in the number of trusts and GP practices to receive care records systems; this meant

---

[180] Yes, it's an acronym. The name of this project management system, rather elliptically, stands for "PRojects IN Controlled Environments" (though the environments in which I've managed projects have seemed quite hard to control).

abandoning the aim of creating an electronic record for all patients, and an unknown impact on the expected benefits overall. Meanwhile the new coalition Government's plans for devolving authority within the NHS introduced new risks that the need for a comprehensive system might disappear altogether, making the whole thing a white elephant. On 3 August 2011 the Public Accounts Committee suggested that the remainder of the programme be cancelled, and the following month the Government took that advice.

Of course, the NHS IT Programme was not typical. At more than £12bn, it was the largest IT project ever undertaken in the UK[181], and subject to a particularly uncontrolled political environment. But actually it points up quite neatly some of the characteristics even of pretty small problem projects. They include:

(i) Optimism in the initial plan;

(ii) A good start;

(iii) New opportunities arise and internal stakeholders demand more;

(iv) The contractor (who may have bid too low so as to land the contract, and cannot afford to keep his promises) delivers less than expected;

(v) Overspend or scope reduction, bringing failure to achieve planned benefits in relation to costs;

(vi) Change in overall strategy before the benefits are fully delivered, adding to the failure in achieving planned returns[182].

---

[181] For comparison, the cuts made to public expenditure in George Osborne's 2010 budget, described (by opponents) as "savage", were £20bn a year, though these were of course recurrent, not one-off.

[182] More specific guidance on IT projects has been given many times (though it is rarely heeded), ranging from Brooks F P Jnr, 1982, *The Mythical Man-Month*, Addison-Wesley, Reading, Mass, to Fishenden J and Thompson M, 2011, *Digital Government, Open Architecture, and Innovation: Why Public Sector IT Will Never Be The Same Again*, http://www.socitm.net/download/1085/digital_government_open_ architecture_and_innovation_why_public_sector_it_will_never_be_the_same_again-mark_thompson_ict_futures_advisor_cabinet_office_plenary_11, downloaded 18

Such problems are notorious in the public sector. But they are just as common in the private sector[183], for the three main differences between the sectors are not in fact material:

- Public services usually have to be given to everyone no matter how complex their needs, which means they need much more complicated systems than do businesses, which can pick and choose their customers.
- Public organisations are generally bigger, so their project failures are more spectacular.
- And public organisations are openly accountable, so their project failures are out on display for the political opposition to savage, while the private sector, where fewer have an interest in washing dirty linen in public, can usually hush them up[184].

Why bang on about project management when our concern is with organisational change? Because the two are, in fact, very closely linked. Most big projects can't be implemented without organisational change. And all organisational change is itself, in effect, a project: it involves moving from one pretty clearly-defined state to another; it requires planning, monitoring and management; and it demands both careful thought at each stage about the consequences and how they should be encouraged or warded off, and also astute improvisation when they are not as anticipated. For change involves the unexpected, and no plan of operations survives contact with the enemy.

January 2011. See also Budzier A and Flyvbjerg B, 2011, *Double Whammy – How ICT Projects are Fooled by Randomness and Screwed by Political Intent*, Saïd Business School working papers, University of Oxford, which looks at 1,471 ICT projects and stresses the part played by optimism bias and by rare but high-impact ("black swan") events.

[183] Budzier A and Flyvbjerg B, 2011 (*op. cit.*), page 4.

[184] A study in 2001 found that only 13% of all Government IT projects, and less than 1% of IT development projects, were successful (Taylor A, 2001, "IT projects sink or swim", *British Computer Society Review*).

The opportunity for a scientific, evidence-based approach to organisational change is unfortunately limited. Change involves action in such complex systems, many reaching into the world outside the organisation where management's writ does not run, that there are few elements of it where robust and transferable conclusions can be reached. There are nevertheless some areas which can be effectively researched, and there is a wealth of useful experience to draw on.

Models of change

There are many models of organisational change: Kurt Lewin's was the earliest popular model, though it is little more than schematic, and more recent favourites are the McKinsey 7S model, Kotter's 8 Step model, and the Burke-Litwin model. These have many common features. They all include:

- management commitment;
- espousing a vision;
- resourcing;
- planning;
- communication; and
- follow-through.

None of these models is "right", though all are reasonable guides, to be either followed meticulously or at least borne in mind as you pick your way through the minefields of reality. What is important is to take all the components seriously: for example, "communication" may sound a bit routine, but it is a real challenge to make sure that the right things about a planned change are effectively communicated to everyone involved, including people outside the organisation; that their views are taken fully on board, and that this is credibly demonstrated; that communication is not just done and then the next thing turned to, but kept on managers' agenda daily as plans move through various iterations and are adjusted for events.

Systems theory can be especially helpful in handling change. Put very crudely, this is a posh term for thinking things through thoroughly: it makes one look further ahead and consider consequences at several removes.

Systems theory was first generalised in 1950 by an Austrian called Bertalanffy[185]. Striding forward from a *Systems thinking* number of ideas then current, he saw that one might take the idea of closed systems in the physical sciences (such as electrical or engineering systems), and apply it much more generally to systems in the biological and social sciences – systems which were self-regulating and open to a changing environment. The systems thinking which is useful in organisations has to do with what are called "complex adaptive systems": "complex" because they look at something which is made up of a number of component systems, each of which is itself self-regulating; and "adaptive" because changes in their environment affect the systems in question, and make them respond in some way (for example to restore their balance, or to reject the change).

Systems thinking encourages one to take into account how various organisational, social and other systems inside and outside an organisation will react to change, and to think out how all the various consequences will work through until stability returns. It tends to involve getting the views of a wider range of stakeholders, looking at problems from a variety of perspectives, trying out different ways of framing problems to find the most useful, expanding their boundaries until the constraints which make them difficult become opportunities for change.

It often feels a bit like psychotherapy, in the sense that the difficulty which seemed so obvious when you started to look at it later almost disappears, as you realise that it was

---

[185] von Bertalanffy, K L, 1950, *An Outline of General System Theory*, British Journal for the Philosophy of Science 1, p. 139-164.

really hiding a much more fundamental problem. Indeed, the parallel pioneers of systems thinking in Britain, at the Tavistock Institute, who called it "sociotechnical systems theory", came at the problem from an explicitly psycho-therapeutic direction[186].

In practice, key results of this will be much greater attention to the constraints and incentives affecting different stakeholders, and also, more generally, to communication, including listening harder to various groups and interests, so as to anticipate and influence responses to interventions. A good example of a systems approach is in a 2002 paper on the NHS by the think-tank DEMOS[187].

Peter Senge, an authoritative adept of systems thinking as a way of addressing organisational changes, has argued that the systems approach is a necessary condition, but not a sufficient one, for successful change in a complex organisation. Also important is leadership vision, which has inspired organizations for thousands of years, can win assent to a shared picture of the future, encourages experimentation and innovation, and above all can foster a helpful sense of the long-term, the reassuring place where the change has already happened[188]. And it is to leadership that we now turn.

---

[186] Although there were many other influences as well, including Kurt Lewin: Jaques E, 1951, *The Changing Culture of a Factory*, Tavistock, &c.
[187] Chapman J, 2002, *System Failure*, Demos, London.
[188] Senge P M, 1990, *The Fifth Discipline: the art and practice of the learning organisation*, Random House, London, pp 9-12.

Chapter 8: Leadership

This chapter surveys how ideas about leadership have developed, and the debate whether one can learn to be a good leader or not. It asks if leadership is different from management, and whether it is better top-down or bottom-up. It looks at the importance of trust and flexibility, the key role of supervisors, and what can be learned from bad leaders.

"...how to grant suits,
How to deny them, who t'advance, and who
To trash for over-topping..."

The Tempest, William Shakespeare, 1611

In truth there wasn't enough for everyone to do, but they turned up anyway, to do it. It was that kind of night. You had to be there, so that later you could say '...and I was there, that very night.' Moist knew he ought to get some sleep, but he had to be there too, alive and sparkling. It was...amazing. They listened to him, they did things for him, they scuttled around as if he was a real leader and not some cheat and fraud.

Going Postal, Terry Pratchett, 2004

What are executives good at? Nothing in particular, really: they are 'generalists'. They have studied in the top colleges such as Political Science and the Central School, where they have not learned much, other than how to impress selection panels. They read newspaper columns written by two or three people who just repeat commonplaces and received ideas, they spice up their talk with simplistic American jargon, and they make this all sound very important. Let's be clear: executives are basically completely uncultured...Our high flyers have never had the time to read Michel Foucault, to listen to a Mozart opera or to watch a Fellini film. Oh, no! Never! They are swamped. By what? By how they spend their time. And how do they spend their time? In meetings...

Bonjour Paresse, Corinne Maier, 2004

"I want to see a quick and tangible return on the investment made in continuous improvement initiatives. This is partly because this measure is used by the Board as the main criterion in assessing my performance."

(senior manager quoted in) Stuck in the Middle with You: the effects of incongruency of senior and middle managers' orientations on TQM programmes, Ebrahim Soltani and Adrian Wilkinson, 2010

Key message of this chapter: Leadership is much studied, but is an art rather than a science, and we are clearer on what is bad leadership than on what is good.

Leadership is a fashionable topic, as we see from the media and our own office gossip. But it almost sums up the problem this book seeks to address: the difficulty of seeing the truth for the mirages.

Looking at the airport bookstalls, one might be forgiven for thinking that every top manager knows the secret of leadership. Bill Gates (Microsoft), Jim Collins (CNN), Richard Branson (Virgin Group), Robert K. Greenleaf (AT&T), Tom Peters (McKinsey), Alan Sugar (Amstrad), Donald Trump (The Trump Organization), Robert H. Waterman Jr (McKinsey), Sir John Harvey Jones (ICI), Jack Welch (General Electric), Andrew Grove (Intel), Steve Wozniak (Apple), Michael Dell (Dell), Fred Smith (FedEx), and hundreds of others have favoured us with their insights. Such books often tend to be written in ways which explain and justify the heroic achievements of these leaders.

But there is a great deal of difference between on the one hand these reminiscences, and on the other robust scientific findings about the effectiveness of leadership. Indeed, there is a great deal of difference between these reminiscences themselves. What are we to make of this?

One might think that it was all down to our celebrity culture. But the truth is that people have been writing stuff like this since Julius Caesar published *On the Gallic War*. The same social instinct that makes us gossip around the coffee machine has always made people enjoy listening to stories and exploring other people's personalities, and there have always been ambitious folk who have realised that getting their own story out there would be to their advantage, whether now or in terms of their legacy.

Again, that is not to say that the stories that leaders tell about their success is wrong. What it does say is that these appealing stories won't necessarily apply to you.

It also explains why leadership is a big issue, in the sense that it has attracted a great deal of attention and there are many different kinds of stories about it, and many important questions, such as:

- Are leaders born, or made: can you learn to be a leader?
- Is there a right and a wrong way of behaving as a leader?
- Does leadership vary between different cultures?
- Do you need different leaders in different situations?
- Is "leadership" the same as "management"?

And if you have been reading this book from the start you will already know what I am going to say next: that a big issue like leadership is full of complexities which it is hard to measure and control for, and that therefore not much of it is capable of being empirically tested.

So what do we really know about leadership? In fact we can be sure of less than the stories of heroic leaders might suggest, and to see how things stand it will help to take a highly condensed tour of the history of the discipline.

Theorising about leadership has a long history, going back to ancient writers like Plutarch in the first century: he *Leader* grappled with the question whether good leaders were born *ship –* or made – still, of course, a live question for organisations. *the* The post-classical world was run by aristocrats, and for a *ground* very long time it preferred explanations that legitimised the idea of inheritance. This remained dominant for a long time, culminating in the Victorian Thomas Carlyle, and in Francis Galton, one of the first to seek to treat psychology as a science.

Thus, attempts in the English civil war and the French revolution to set inheritance aside proved damp squibs. It was not until after the Second World War that there was a serious challenge, when Nazism had discredited the hitherto widely popular idea of racial differences, and with it all but the most robust ideas about heritable characteristics. At this time Stogdill and others were able to gain wide acceptance for evidence that leadership depended not on *character traits* consistently linked with success, but on its *environ-*

ment – the leader's skills, organisation, situation, and followers. Since the 1980s, trait-based theories have fought back, especially with a (slightly desperate?) argument that it is packages of traits rather than individual traits which assure success. However, this may be a bit of a smoke-screen: the situation remains uncertain, and no school of thought has yet been able to declare its opponents' paradigm defunct.

This question is a fundamental one. If permanent characteristics are what determines leadership success, then there is a limited supply of leaders, and choosing the right ones is possible and vital. If not, then leadership skills are learnable: anyone can be a leader, and the requisite skills may vary from case to case. There is probably room for compromise between these two polar positions; but in general my own vote (and I think the balance of current psychological opinion) goes for the conclusion that it is learnable rather than inherited.

However, there are two other basic questions which are also fundamental to what one thinks about leadership: (i) is there a difference between "leadership" and "management"?; and (ii) is leadership a matter of telling other people what to do, or enabling them to do things on their own initiative?

Leadership and management "Leadership" and "management" used to be fairly inter-changeable terms, until there was a move in the 1960s to separate them out. This led to the latter soon seeming to recall the deadening "science of management" invented by Frederick Taylor; while the former became able to evoke more exciting questions like what brings success in kingship and battles. Thus, in practice, management became seen as being, rather boringly, about the nuts-and-bolts aspects of control and decision-making, such as project plans, Gantt charts, call centre scripts and record-keeping. Leadership, on the other hand, was seen as being, much more dramatically, about inspiration, creativity, insight, loyalty and daring to do the impossible.

It is curious that "management" had such a bad press. For it remains the case that an awful lot of what executives actually do is setting up and enforcing complicated procedures to ensure that things are done right; indeed, the advent of ISO quality mechanisms, call centre scripting and other automated processes has meant that this is in fact an even bigger part of the job than it was in the past, and is vitally important in the way organisations are now run. But the word "leadership", of course, won the unequal contest between the two terms. Indeed, the pair have now been repackaged as "transformational leadership" and "transactional leadership"[189]; this neatly sidesteps the question of whether there is a real difference between the two words. However, it does remain the case that things have to be organised if inspirations are to be delivered, and that a group of people needs a vision of where they are going even if their systems, records and procedures are already impeccably well sorted out.

Whether leadership should be authoritarian or participative was another issue much affected by fascism and the Second World War. We have seen that in the Edwardian era there was great enthusiasm for Taylor's idea of Scientific Management, in which the Manager would decide how work was to be done, and the Worker would do as he was told. But, be that as it may, in the years following Auschwitz management writers felt duty bound to show that autocratic leadership styles were unsuccessful.

Authoritarian & participative leadership

And their thoughts were able to reach a wide audience. Douglas McGregor advocated what he called Theory Y[190],

---

[189] Since Burns J McG, 1978, *Leadership*. Note especially Bass B M, 1985, Leadership and performance beyond expectation. New York : Free Press.

[190] McGregor D, 1960, *The Human Side of the Enterprize*, McGraw-Hill, New York.

and Rensis Likert what he called System 4[191] – in each case arguing, on the basis of rather thin research evidence, for job enlargement, participative leadership and decentralisation of power. A fuller theoretical base for this was devised by Chris Argyris, who argued that as people grew to true adulthood they acquired an autonomy which was incompatible with the dependency demanded by authoritarian management styles[192]. It's interesting that no serious attempt was made by these authors to see how these ideas stacked up in a non-Euroamerican context, for example in the economic ebullience of Japan, Taiwan and South Korea, where quite different studies of cultural norms were at the same time suggesting that individual initiative was much less valued than in the USA[193].

Moreover, the extent to which enthusiasm for participative leadership has actually made much difference to leadership practice is open to question. Command-and-control styles are alive and well all over the place[194], and even leaders who do not choose to use such a style may revert to it under pressure[195].

Most of the more influential subsequent interventions on leadership have been variations on these themes. Participative leadership has increasingly been looked at with the aid of ideas of "followership": an understanding that people being led can develop their ability to participate in

---

[191] Likert R, 1970, "New Patterns of Management", in Vroom V H and Deci E L, *Management and Motivation*, Penguin Books, Harmondsworth.

[192] Argyris C, 1957, *Personality and Organisation*, Harper and Row, New York.

[193] Hofstede G, 2001, *Culture's Consequences: comparing values, behaviors, institutions, and organizations across nations* (2nd ed.), Thousand Oaks, CA, Sage Publications, ISBN 978-0-8039-7323-7; Trompenaars F, and Hampden-Turner C, 1997, *Riding The Waves of Culture: Understanding Diversity in Global Business*. Argyris had wisely pointed out that his argument was culturally restricted, though he did not develop the implications of this; certainly its assumptions look to be a good deal more fragile outside the suburban United States and northern Europe.

[194] Evan Rosen cited in *Performance Preview*, pub Ernst and Young, May 2011 p. 9.

[195] Dotlich D L and Cairo P C, 2002, *Unnatural Leadership: going against intuition and experience to develop ten new leadership instincts*, Jossey-Bass, San Francisco.

decision-making rather than just do as they are told, and that successful leaders are able to pitch their leadership style so as to be attuned to (i) their own personality strengths, (ii) the situation and character of the group they lead, and (iii) the maturity of followership achieved by its members[196]. Participative leadership probably reached its peak with the idea of the leader's role being in the service of the group being led, or "servant leadership"[197].

Studies of leadership tend to focus on the top leaders. This is possibly because researchers themselves get better lunches and more pay in such work. But it is also because top leaders are seen as very powerful. There is in psychology something called rather impenetrably the "fundamental attribution error": it means that people prefer to give personal explanations for other people's behaviour, rather than looking to situational causes for it. This means that we tend to see changes as being made by people on purpose, rather than simply being the outcome of impersonal market forces (which may be why it is easier to get an idea across by telling a story than by delivering a dry analysis). *Celebrity leaders*

Thus a study of American press reports (and other evidence) in the 1970s found that when firms were doing very well or badly, rather than just coasting along, people were more likely to attribute this to the Chief Executive's doing, than to the market, or to an entrenched organisational culture, or to any other abstract imponderable which might

---

[196] Fiedler F E, 1967, A theory of leadership effectiveness, NY: McGraw-Hill; Hersey P & Blanchard K, 1972, Management of Organizational Behavior: Utilizing Human Resources, Englewood Cliffs NJ: Prentice Hall.

[197] Greenleaf R K, 1977, Servant-Leadership: A journey into the nature of legitimate power and greatness, Mahwah, NJ : Paulist Press (mind you, servant leadership is not a new idea, the Popes having described themselves as "servant of the servants of God" since the sixth century, though it is food for thought that this has apparently not been incompatible with a lot of authoritarian behaviour by the Papacy, especially in the late middle ages).

seem on reflection pretty likely to be the real influence at work[198].

There will always be enthusiasm for formulas offering magical hope of improvement. And even people who are bright enough to spot that they are unlikely to win the Euro-lottery often fasten on their own character as something they may be more likely to control than the outside world. Hence nostrums such as Stephen Covey's self-help book *Seven Habits of Highly Effective People*, which sprang in 1989 from a soil made up mainly of Mormonism and the American Dream. It sold over 15 million copies, for it came at the right time: the 1990s saw a revival and burgeoning of the idea of the heroic transformational leader who drove the success of a company by his genius alone. Turbulent economic fortunes, of course, have now tarnished this model, which has often been overtaken by ideas of partici-pative or distributed leadership[199].

Like organisational change, leadership is action in a very complex environment, often full of organisational politics, where those aspects capable of being properly measured and controlled for are relatively limited. The real consequences of leadership actions, as a result, are hard to predict. So, like change, it is an area where science can make a contribution, but where informed good judgement is often the best guide. There are several theoretical

---

[198] Meindl J R, Ehrlich S B, Dukerich J M, 1985, "The romance of leadership", *Administrative Science Quarterly*, vol 30 pp 78-102.

[199] Collins J argued that the "hero-leader" is an unstable though highly successful model (2001, *Good to Great*, Random House, London, p. 46: "the towering genius, the primary driving force in the company's success, is a great asset, so long as the genius sticks around"); see also Morrow I J, *Defining a New Type of Organizational Leadership: The Heroic Leader*, 1999, Faculty Working Papers: Paper 22 http://digitalcommons.pace.edu/lubinfaculty_workingpapers/22; Ainsworth P, 2009, *No more heroes? Does collaboration spell the death of the heroic leader?*, National College for School Leadership, Nottingham. See in addition Goffee R and Jones G, 2000, "Why should anyone be led by you?", *Harvard Business Review*, September.

approaches which offer useful insights, but none which is manifestly superior.

A great deal of effort has been put into trying to spot personal characteristics that make for good leaders. This has come up with answers ranging from dominance to masculinity, and from extraversion to technical know-ledge[200]; conscientiousness has also been linked to leadership success[201]. *Is there a formula?*

However, it cannot be said that there are very consistent results from such studies, though we need not go so far as one recent survey of the leadership literature, which concluded that it was "...a strange mixture of alchemy, romantic idealism, and reason", and found that the lack of consistent, actionable findings prompted business people "...to wash their hands of the whole subject, talent shortage or no talent shortage."[202]. It is important to get the focus right. Probably the most authoritative study found as long ago as 1948 that, while there are a few high-level common factors among leaders – who do tend to be relatively more intelligent, educated, vigorous, and high up the class ladder – it is not innate personality characteristics that make for good leadership[203]. The truth seems to be that the kind of leadership needed varies from organisation to organi-

---

[200] Stogdill R M, 1974, *Handbook of Leadership: A Survey of Theory and Research*, New York, Free Press; House R J and Baetz M L, 1979, "Leadership: some empirical generalisations and new research directions" – in B M Staw (ed.), *Research in Organizational Behavior*, Greenwich USA, J.A.I. Press; Mann R D, 1959, "A review of the relationships between personality and performance in small groups", *Psychological Bulletin*, Vol 56(4), Jul, 241-270; Schaumberg R, & Flynn F, 2012, "Uneasy Lies the Head That Wears the Crown: The Link Between Guilt Proneness and Leadership", *Journal of Personality and Social Psychology*.

[201] van Iddekinge C *et al.*, "Test of a Multistage Model of Distal and Proximal Antecedents of Leader Performance", *Personnel Psychology*, 2009 vol. 62 pp 463-495.

[202] Kramer R J, 2008, "Have we learned anything about leadership development?", *Conference Board Review, 45*, pp 26-30: a short but influential contribution.

[203] Stogdill R M, 1948, "Personal factors associated with leadership", *Journal of Psychology*, 23 35-71; Kramer 2008, without citing an evidence base, comes to similar conclusions.

sation and from situation to situation; and that in most cases a range of individuals can provide it.

How to recognise what skills match what situations is still debated. The key focus for a long time was on whether in a particular case a leader needed to focus his or her action on production or employees, since it was argued that the former was essential to maximise production capacity, at least in manufacturing firms, while the latter was a key to unlocking discretionary staff effort[204]. Yet a study in 1978 identified as many as 14 variables that might usefully be consulted, and the discussion continues to this day[205].

So the answer may be not so much choosing the right leader, as for the leader chosen to adopt the right leadership style for the situation. There are, however, at least as yet, no agreed ground rules about what style might be right for a particular case, so that this choice must simply be left to the intuition of the leader.

That said, there is a fair amount of agreement that that style has to be one with which he or she can be comfortable, and good training for leaders can therefore achieve a great deal, addressing issues such as authenticity, which is always important in leadership, as well as more technical skills such as communication. We have seen how important people's trust in their organisation is, if they are to respect their unwritten contract with their employer, and how crucial in maintaining it is the behaviour of senior leaders (page 51). Personal contact with managers is vital for staff, as it enables them to use verbal and non-verbal cues to judge their sincerity and the worth of the messages they are

---

[204] Steiner I D, 1976, "Task-performing groups", in Thibaut J W, Spence J T and Carson R C (eds), *Contemporary Topics in Social Psychology*, General Learning Press, Morristown NJ USA.

[205] Kerr S and Jernier J M, 1978, "Substitutes for Leadership: their meaning and measurement", *Organizational Behavior and Human Performance*, vol. 22 pp. 375-403.

giving: bosses who hide in their office, sending out reams of written managerialist gobbledegook, will carry no conviction, and will damage morale and motivation[206].

There may also be cultural factors involved, and managers of multicultural teams will need to be alert to this. Research in this area is not far advanced. Current indications are that resourcefulness and relationship skills are highly valued in managers across different cultures. Work-life balance skills, however, seem to vary greatly, being valued very little in Russia, and only moderately in Austria, Hong Kong, Japan, Taiwan and the UK, while they are much more highly thought of in Indonesia, Malaysia, the Philippines, Thailand, Australia, New Zealand and Colombia[207].

In recent years an important contribution to this debate has been made by turning the problem on its head, and trying to work out not what makes for good leaders, but what makes for poor ones[208]. For bad leaders are very costly: large US organisations have estimated the cost of a failed senior manager at over $1m, not counting the effect on their colleagues' and subordinates' morale, stress and motivation; and it has been suggested (admittedly by someone with a vested interest in psychometric tests which might be useful if it were true) "that two thirds of existing

Bad leader-ship

---

[206] Hope-Hailey V, Searle R and Dietz G , 2012, *Where has all the trust gone?*, CIPD, Wimbledon p 15;

[207] Gentry W A and Sparks T E, 2012, "A Convergence/Divergence Perspective of Leadership Competencies Managers Believe are Most Important for Success in Organizations: A Cross-Cultural Multilevel Analysis of 40 Countries", *Journal of Business Psychology*, vol 27 pp 15-30.

[208] The model text here is Hogan J, Hogan R and Kaiser R B, 2010, "Managerial Derailment", in Zedeck S, 2010, *APA Handbook of Industrial and Organizational Psychology*, American Psychological Association, Washington DC, USA, vol 3 cap 15.

managers are insufferable and that half will eventually fail"[209].

The main problems shown by poor leaders (in war, as well as in organisations) vary between studies, but are chiefly around interpersonal issues such as sensitivity to others, tact, political skills, dealing with conflict, weak emotional control, indecision, procrastination, and poor team-building (also to some extent around over-concern with detail, difficulties in adopting strategic change, selfishness and poor performance management). Research has, as usual, mostly been in the USA, but has reached similar results in Belgium, France, Germany, Italy, Spain and the UK[210].

These weaknesses, though falling within the range of normal personality and not strong enough to get them classed as personality disorders, are rather sensationally referred to by psychologists as "the dark side". Most of them are ones which we all to some extent share, and which only become a problem when taken to excess. However, it is argued that they are often concealed early in someone's career, and that they are more likely actually to become manifested in *senior* managers, because these may risk less by being rather more self-indulgent in their managerial behaviour, and are also subject to greater job pressures which can more often drive them to let down their emotional guard.

The fact that such problems seem to be so widely shared means that the issue cannot be addressed, collectively at least, by trying to select people who are altogether without them. There simply would not be enough of these, so such an approach would be a perfectionist mistake.

Training is a better answer, since simply improving managers' self-awareness is likely to help them to correct

---

[209] Hogan &c 2010, p. 3.
[210] Hogan &c 2010, pp. 5-10.

the impact of these weaknesses for themselves[211]. People form habits of thought and behaviour in order to minimise the effort involved in dealing with repeated situations[212]. Such habits then become hard to break without conscious effort. But with help, reflection and practice, this can be done.

However, habits may have become so embedded that a lot of introspection is needed to bring them to the level of awareness needed. And work of this sort can go well beyond what most busy managers would expect of management coaching, and into the borders of psychotherapeutic counselling – which they may well resist, thinking that it implies a sickness or eccentricity which they do not experience and which it would be imprudent to acknowledge in a work context.

Another way of improving self-awareness is through 360° feedback, in which managers receive regular reports on their performance not just from their own line manager but from their colleagues at similar and more junior levels. This is an important tool, not least because poor leaders are often a good deal worse at managing their subordinates than at managing upwards (indeed, grooming their own managers may be what got them to where they are). Hence a good 360° feedback approach will often open up key issues which might otherwise fester throughout a career[213]. However, it does need to be properly administered, since a number of pitfalls can open up if it is done on the cheap.

An area of management which deserves special attention is first-line managers or supervisors. These are

---

[211] Though it is not yet clear whether this is true, or usefully true, of everyone.

[212] Douglas M, 1986, *How Institutions Think*, Routledge, London; see also Iyengar S S & Kamenica E, 2010, "Choice proliferation, simplicity seeking, and asset allocation", *Journal of Public Economics*, 94(7), 530-539.

[213] Kaplan R E, Drath W H and Kofodimos J R, 1991, *Beyond Ambition*, Jossey-Bass, San Francisco.

people whose role is described by the anthropologists as "liminal", meaning that they are not quite wholly managers and not quite wholly workers, but on the boundary, sometimes one and sometimes the other, which is an uncomfortable place to be.

Junior mana- gers
Only one major study before the Second World War looked at the relationship between productivity levels and first-line supervisors: it found that there was one, but not why[214]. Subsequently, a good deal of effort was put at an Institute of Social Research in Michigan into leadership styles at first-line supervisor level; it suggested, satisfactorily in the post-war context, that autocratic styles were less successful than more participative ones.

However, by the 1950s it was emerging that there had been problems with the methods used in these studies, and that the true position was rather more complicated. For example, more autonomous groups were not necessarily more productive; whether supervisors adopted a parti- cipative style was often dependent not so much on their own skills or aptitudes, as on whether top management was sympathetic or not; and what was cause and what was effect were often rather arguable[215]. However, first-line super- visors are now back in fashion again[216], following recognition that their role has grown with technical and organisational changes such as delayering[217].

This is largely because supervisors are responsible for implementing staff management policies. In some large organisations this role drifted over to HR in the late 20th

---

[214] Feldman H, 1937, *Problems in Labor Relations,* Macmillan, New York.

[215] Rose M, 1975, *Industrial Behaviour: theoretical development since Taylor,* Penguin Books, Harmondsworth pp 163-166.

[216] eg Hales C, 2005, "Rooted in Supervision, Branching into Management: Continuity and Change in the Role of First-Line Manager", *Journal of Management Studies* Vol 42, Issue 3, pages 471-506; see also "In Praise of David Brent", *Economist,* 27 August 2011 p. 58.

[217] Kerr S, Hill K D, Broedling L, 1986, "The First-Line Supervisor: phasing out or here to stay?", *Academy of Management Review,* 1986, pp 103-117.

century, and may now seem rather a new task for line management; but, of course, this would be misleading, and it is a core part of the job. Supervisors are able to do much by example, for instance by carrying out appraisals enthusiastically and creatively instead of perfunctorily, or by making the effort to coach and enthuse their team. They can do the job of local leadership well, by being fair and open and consistent, by listening to their team and consulting them before making decisions, by judging sensibly when they need to supervise closely and when they can delegate. They should also feed their teams' views back to middle and senior management, so that the latter understand the impact of their own actions on the morale of the employees.

There is a loose package of people-management policies which has acquired the description of "HR policies and practices"[218]. The recent Purcell study of performance[219] has shown a good correlation between satisfaction with front-line leadership and such management policies, especially involvement, "respect shown by my line manager", communication and openness; and this was mostly tied in with a sense of commitment to the organisation. The case studies in this work showed some evidence, following expansion of the line manager role, of recruitment difficulties being eased and of praise becoming a new and material motivator. This reinforces in today's world long-standing evidence for the importance of the part played by line managers in motivating employees.

"Human resource management" practices

Above all, perhaps, supervisors have a key role in modelling actions for their teams. For example, in nearly all

---

[218] Originally these were techniques designed to evade management-union confrontation through co-opting employee commitment to managerial goals: various quality initiatives, integration of personnel policies into strategic business planning, job flexibility, and non-union works councils (Millward N, 1994, *The New Industrial Relations?*, Policy Studies Institute, London, p 3); though quality is still on the list, the emphasis now tends to be around communication, involvement/delegation and skills acquisition (Purcell &c 2003 p 41).

[219] See page 53.

jobs, there are things you are told you have to do (the specified content), and other things which it would be useful to do (the discretionary content) – such as doing things a bit faster, or deciding what ought to be done in situations which your instructions don't cover. The main difference between good performance and adequate performance is that good performance has lots of discretionary content (although the strengthening of work standardisation, as briefly described on page 57, does tend to have narrowed the opportunities for it). A good supervisor will show his team that he himself does discretionary things, and will also encourage them to do discretionary things in their own jobs[220].

The recent Hope-Hailey study[221] examined various patterns of trust in organisations and concluded that trust in line managers was the most resilient kind of trust relationship. It warned, however, that first-line supervisors, if abandoned by managers preoccupied with other crises, could easily "go native", so that it was vital to make sure they understood the corporate strategy and behaved in tune with it[222]. The motivation and commitment of supervisors was looked at in the Purcell work, which found that provision of training and career opportunities, along with support from their own line managers, was crucial to sustain them[223].

Consistency in the signals sent by senior management is vital for this. Work on why 60%-90% of quality initiatives fail has suggested that this is often down to short-termism. Consider this example. Typically, senior managers seek to impress directors by launching a quality improvement drive (for example by getting production right first time instead of relying on quality checks to identify errors). They are then

---

[220] Purcell J, Kinnie N, Hutchinson S, Rayton B and Swart J, 2003, *Understanding the People and Performance Link: unlocking the black box*, CIPD London, pp 37-49.
[221] See page 51.
[222] Hope-Hailey R, Searle R and Dietz G, 2012, *Where has all the trust gone?*, CIPD, Wimbledon pp 22, 34-35.
[223] Purcell J, Kinnie N, Hutchinson S, Rayton B and Swart J, 2003, *op.cit.*, pp 67-68.

pushed to improve short-term results (in the private sector, generally financial ones; elsewhere, often KPIs of some sort), and this has to be done by renewed emphasis on quality checks, diverting resource from the process improvements which were to bring about better initial production[224]. Junior managers, meanwhile, who have been acquiring quality skills (such as encouraging team autonomy and devolving their own authority), will then find this coming back to bite them as they are suddenly expected to deliver better old-style results, hindered by their bewildered teams who now feel empowered to challenge the new instructions. The new way of working has no time to bed down, and instead staff are worked harder in the old way[225]. The result is not at all satisfactory for anyone.

There is one additional matter here. A fair amount of work has been done on leadership teams, which suggests that analysis of team roles can be of importance in this area. *Teams* Two team role analysis systems are in common use[226], and their publishers make various claims for them, including that they identify several functions required to tackle projects (such as initiator, ideas person, co-ordinator, completer, auditor), and can be used to ensure that teams are not made up in ways which miss out key roles or skills.

These claims have not been borne out by robust independent tests[227], but in practice users seem to find that

---

[224] Soltani E and Wilkinson A, 2010, "Stuck in the Middle with You: the effects of incongruency of senior and middle managers' orientations on TQM programmes", *International Journal of Operations and Production Management*, vol 30 no 4 pp 365-397.

[225] See also Kerr S, 1995, "On the folly of rewarding A, while hoping for B", *Academy of Management Executive*; vol 9, issue 1; pg. 7 (originally published 1975: reprinted by popular demand).

[226] These are the Belbin Team-Role Self-Perception Inventory and the Margerison-McCann Team Management System.

[227] See for example Furnham A, Steele H and Pendleton D, 1993, "A Psychometric assessment of the Belbin Team-Role Self-Perception Inventory", *Journal of Occupational and Organizational Psychology*, vol. 66, pp. 245-257; Fisher S G.,

the approach carries a fair amount of conviction. However, you cannot look at ideas like this too mechanically, not least because a chief officer who has a particular team role on the main board will also have quite a different team role elsewhere – on the board he might be the ideas person, but in his own department he will probably have a chairing/leadership/co-ordinating role. So he needs to be able to perform *both* roles effectively…

Leadership involves a lot of fire-fighting, and so is by nature an activity liable to distraction. This is an essential characteristic of the task and cannot be eliminated. But many managers are swamped by it. Half the activities engaged in by the five Chief Executives in one major study lasted less than nine minutes, and only 10% exceeded one hour; while work on 56 U.S. foremen found that they averaged 583 activities per eight-hour shift, an average of one every 48 seconds[228].

It is unsurprising that many find it hard to take purposeful action as a result. So it is essential that organisations take what opportunities there are to support their leaders' focus, through for example mentoring, coaching, emotional support and accountability processes[229].

Planning can be a help or a hindrance here. The term is used to cover a set of rather different activities: plans can range from disciplined bureaucratic devices needed to make sure things happen the right way with the right resources at the right time, to feelgood portraits of a desired future; and

---

Macrosson W D K and Sharp G, 1996, "Further evidence concerning the Belbin Team-Role Self-Perception Inventory", *Personnel Review*, vol 25 no 2, pp 61-67.
[228] Mintzberg H, 1975, "The Manager's Job: Folklore and Fact", *Harvard Business Review*, July-August 1975.
[229] Ghoshal S and Bruch H, *A Bias for Action*, Harvard Business School Press, 2004; Ghoshal S and Bruch H, 2010, "Management is the art of doing and getting done", *Business Strategy Review*, London Business School, Q2 issue, pp 70-75.

they can have timescales ranging from a week or two, to decades into the future.

Nothing happens without a plan of some sort, but large organisations frequently squander vast amounts of resource on maintaining plans which are constantly rewritten yet which nobody ever seems to refer to or use. As with so many other aspects of organisational life, plans need to be tailored sensitively to their purpose and context, and jettisoned when their usefulness is over. There is no more than a smidgen of truth in the suggestion that it is the process of planning rather than the plan itself which has value. A good plan, well put together with the commitment of all involved, and then executed with care, attention and common sense, is an invaluable guide to action. And action is a part of organisational life to which we next turn.

Chapter 9: Action

You may be reading this book with a particular people-management problem in mind. If so, you need to watch that you do not jump to conclusions about what is needed. Organisations are littered with managers who instinctively knew how a problem ought to be resolved, and who are now anxiously trying to clear up the mess before they can be identified as responsible.

Hence it is essential to think through an apparent problem to its real causes before action is taken. This is sometimes easier for someone who is not already involved and has preconceptions which may be misleading; that can be a good reason for getting in outside consultants, or at least a fresh light on the problem from a colleague elsewhere in the organisation.

What sort of new things might you do to reflect what this book shows? You might try using formal management techniques rather more, and relying less on instinct and "common sense". A key one might be getting your staff to fill in anonymous questionnaires: understanding how your staff really feel about their work, their colleagues and you can be a bit scary, but they will give you credit for your courage in doing it, and it can be very powerful when it comes to working out how to motivate them.

However, be careful. Surveys can have some serious shortcomings. A substantial study in 2010 of how people filled in screen-based surveys found that 6% of respondents made, after they had started on the questionnaire, unconvincing changes to opinions they had given earlier, while 46% clicked through at least some parts of the form at a questionably fast rate, and 3% even changed their reported age. They also found that people with these suspicious behaviours also tended to give answers that did not match information got by another route[230]. So if surveys are to be relied on they do need to be cannily designed.

Another initiative which might be worthwhile would be a formal quality assessment method, such as the European Foundation for Quality Management business excellence model, or the Investors in People standard. This would provide a structured way of identifying strengths and weaknesses, and hence point to where additional skills development or other effort would best pay off.

Motivation is a key area, and clarity of goals for all individuals and teams will do more than anything else to ensure engagement. Hence getting appraisal and supervision systems right is essential. Planning is a vital part of this; but it is easy to let "strategy" become a self-seeking activity without much grounding in the real world, so it needs to be kept on tap (as they say), not on top[231].

With luck, this book will have given the reader a better feel for how much we really know about how to manage people, and what he or she should expect about how reliable management decisions ought to be. One thing which is striking is that the areas where we are pretty confident that our decisions are good ones are rather circumscribed. Another is that, in the other more uncertain areas, views of the best approach have varied quite markedly over time, for no very good reason other than shifts in the background climate of opinion about what happens in the world, and in the personal intuition of the more prominent experts.

If you are a practising manager, you have a very difficult job (as you well know), and I hope that the advice in this

---

[230] Stieger S, & Reips U, 2010, "What are participants doing while filling in an online questionnaire: A paradata collection tool and an empirical study", *Computers in Human Behavior,* 26 (6), 1488-1495.

[231] A sound discussion of the proper role of strategy, embedded in a thick discussion of its relationship with many other organisational techniques and qualities, remains in Kay J, 1993, *Foundations of Corporate Success,* OUP, Oxford.

book will help, at least a bit. On the other hand, you also have a job which is very exciting, very involving, and (if you are lucky enough for things to go reasonably well) very satisfying too: you ought to be envied for it.

I ask you to keep an eye on the slow progress of the psychologists, as they gradually sort out more about what works at work. And I wish you good luck and a good intuition in handling the stuff that we really don't yet fully understand.